Offensive Security Certified Complete Self-Assessment Guide

The guidance in this Self-Assessment is based on Offensive Security Certified Professional best practices and standards in business process architecture, design and quality management. The guidance is also based on the professional judgment of the individual collaborators listed in the Acknowledgments.

Notice of rights

Trademarks

Copyright © by The Art of Service
http://theartofservice.com
service@theartofservice.com

Table of Contents

About The Art of Service

The Art of Service, Business Process Architects since 2000, is dedicated to helping stakeholders achieve excellence.

Defining, designing, creating, and implementing a process to solve a stakeholders challenge or meet an objective is the most valuable role… In EVERY group, company, organization and department.

Unless you're talking a one-time, single-use project, there should be a process. Whether that process is managed and implemented by humans, AI, or a combination of the two, it needs to be designed by someone with a complex enough perspective to ask the right questions.

Someone capable of asking the right questions and step back and say, 'What are we really trying to accomplish here? And is there a different way to look at it?'

With The Art of Service's Standard Requirements Self-Assessments, we empower people who can do just that — whether their title is marketer, entrepreneur, manager, salesperson, consultant, Business Process Manager, executive assistant, IT Manager, CIO etc... —they are the people who rule the future. They are people who watch the process as it happens, and ask the right questions to make the process work better.

Contact us when you need any support with this Self-Assessment and any help with templates, blue-prints and examples of standard documents you might need:

http://theartofservice.com
service@theartofservice.com

Acknowledgments

This checklist was developed under the auspices of The Art of Service, chaired by Gerardus Blokdyk.

Representatives from several client companies participated in the preparation of this Self-Assessment.

In addition, we are thankful for the design and printing services provided.

Included Resources - how to access

Included with your purchase of the book is the Offensive Security Certified Professional Self-Assessment Spreadsheet Dashboard which contains all questions and Self-Assessment areas and auto-generates insights, graphs, and project RACI planning - all with examples to get you started right away.

How? Simply send an email to
access@theartofservice.com
with this books' title in the subject to get the Offensive Security Certified Professional Self Assessment Tool right away.

You will receive the following contents with New and Updated specific criteria:

- The latest quick edition of the book in PDF

- The latest complete edition of the book in PDF, which criteria correspond to the criteria in...

- The Self-Assessment Excel Dashboard, and...

- Example pre-filled Self-Assessment Excel Dashboard to get familiar with results generation

- In-depth specific Checklists covering the topic

- Project management checklists and templates to assist with implementation

INCLUDES LIFETIME SELF ASSESSMENT UPDATES

Every self assessment comes with Lifetime Updates and Lifetime Free Updated Books. Lifetime Updates is an industry-first feature which allows you to receive verified self assessment updates, ensuring you always have the most accurate information at your fingertips.

Get it now- you will be glad you did - do it now, before you forget.

Send an email to **access@theartofservice.com** with this books' title in the subject to get the Offensive Security Certified Professional Self Assessment Tool right away.

Your feedback is invaluable to us

If you recently bought this book, we would love to hear from you! You can do this by writing a review on amazon (or the online store where you purchased this book) about your last purchase! As part of our continual service improvement process, we love to hear real client experiences and feedback.

How does it work?
To post a review on Amazon, just log in to your account and click on the Create Your Own Review button (under Customer Reviews) of the relevant product page. You can find examples of product reviews in Amazon. If you purchased from another online store, simply follow their procedures.

What happens when I submit my review?
Once you have submitted your review, send us an email at review@theartofservice.com with the link to your review so we can properly thank you for your feedback.

Purpose of this Self-Assessment

This Self-Assessment has been developed to improve understanding of the requirements and elements of Offensive Security Certified Professional, based on best practices and standards in business process architecture, design and quality management.

It is designed to allow for a rapid Self-Assessment to determine how closely existing management practices and procedures correspond to the elements of the Self-Assessment.

The criteria of requirements and elements of Offensive Security Certified Professional have been rephrased in the format of a Self-Assessment questionnaire, with a seven-criterion scoring system, as explained in this document.

In this format, even with limited background knowledge of Offensive Security Certified Professional, a manager can quickly review existing operations to determine how they measure up to the standards. This in turn can serve as the starting point of a 'gap analysis' to identify management tools or system elements that might usefully be implemented in the organization to help improve overall performance.

How to use the Self-Assessment

On the following pages are a series of questions to identify to what extent your Offensive Security Certified Professional initiative is complete in comparison to the requirements set in standards.

To facilitate answering the questions, there is a space in front of each question to enter a score on a scale of '1' to '5'.

1 Strongly Disagree

2 Disagree

3 Neutral

4 Agree

5 Strongly Agree

Read the question and rate it with the following in front of mind:

**'In my belief,
the answer to this question is clearly defined'.**

There are two ways in which you can choose to interpret this statement;
   1.   how aware are you that the answer to the question is

clearly defined
2. for more in-depth analysis you can choose to gather evidence and confirm the answer to the question. This obviously will take more time, most Self-Assessment users opt for the first way to interpret the question and dig deeper later on based on the outcome of the overall Self-Assessment.

A score of '1' would mean that the answer is not clear at all, where a '5' would mean the answer is crystal clear and defined. Leave emtpy when the question is not applicable or you don't want to answer it, you can skip it without affecting your score. Write your score in the space provided.

After you have responded to all the appropriate statements in each section, compute your average score for that section, using the formula provided, and round to the nearest tenth. Then transfer to the corresponding spoke in the Offensive Security Certified Professional Scorecard on the second next page of the Self-Assessment.

Your completed Offensive Security Certified Professional Scorecard will give you a clear presentation of which Offensive Security Certified Professional areas need attention.

Offensive Security Certified Professional Scorecard Example

Example of how the finalized Scorecard can look like:

Offensive Security Certified Professional Scorecard

Your Scores:

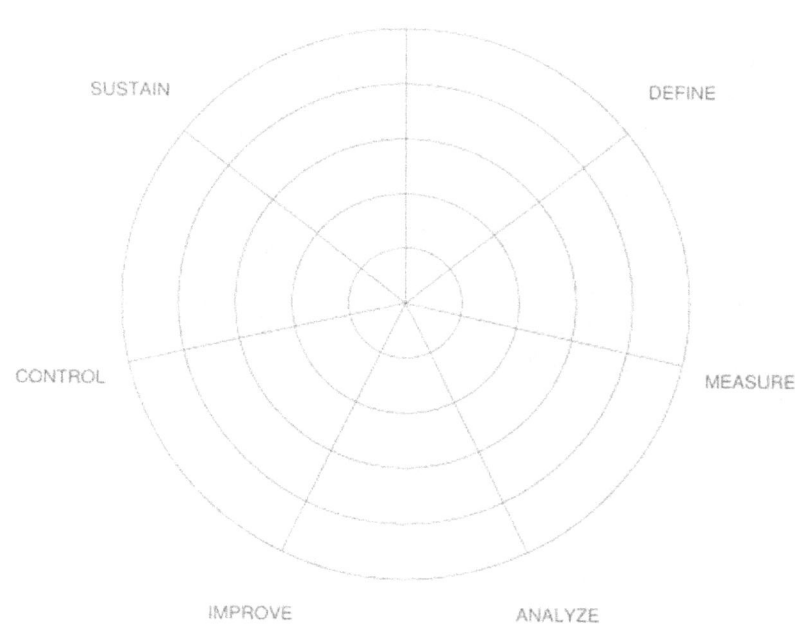

BEGINNING OF THE SELF-ASSESSMENT:

CRITERION #1: RECOGNIZE

INTENT: Be aware of the need for change. Recognize that there is an unfavorable variation, problem or symptom.

In my belief, the answer to this question is clearly defined:

5 Strongly Agree

4 Agree

3 Neutral

2 Disagree

1 Strongly Disagree

1. Does Offensive Security Certified Professional create potential expectations in other areas that need to be recognized and considered?
<--- Score

2. During what time window will testing need to be performed?
<--- Score

3. Are controls defined to recognize and contain problems?
<--- Score

4. Will it solve real problems?
<--- Score

5. Are there any legacy systems that have known issues with automated scanning?
<--- Score

6. What are the stakeholder objectives to be achieved with Offensive Security Certified Professional?
<--- Score

7. What vendors make products that address the Offensive Security Certified Professional needs?
<--- Score

8. Consider your own Offensive Security Certified Professional project. what types of organizational problems do you think might be causing or affecting your problem, based on the work done so far?
<--- Score

9. For your Offensive Security Certified Professional project, identify and describe the business environment. is there more than one layer to the business environment?
<--- Score

10. Who else hopes to benefit from it?
<--- Score

11. Do you participate in industry events and

share information about cyber threats?
<--- Score

12. Is it a configuration problem?
<--- Score

13. How can auditing be a preventative security measure?
<--- Score

14. Can physical components be added or deleted from the system in order to prevent or alter its proper operation?
<--- Score

15. As a sponsor, customer or management, how important is it to meet goals, objectives?
<--- Score

16. What problems are you facing and how do you consider Offensive Security Certified Professional will circumvent those obstacles?
<--- Score

17. Who needs to know about Offensive Security Certified Professional ?
<--- Score

18. Can Management personnel recognize the monetary benefit of Offensive Security Certified Professional?
<--- Score

19. Do we know what we need to know about this topic?
<--- Score

20. What do we need to start doing?
<--- Score

21. Will Offensive Security Certified Professional
deliverables need to be tested and, if so, by whom?
<--- Score

22. What are the expected benefits of Offensive
Security Certified Professional to the stakeholder?
<--- Score

**23. What happens when an identifier greater than
eight characters is used?**
<--- Score

24. Will a response program recognize when a crisis
occurs and provide some level of response?
<--- Score

25. How are you going to measure success?
<--- Score

**26. Think about the people you identified for your
Offensive Security Certified Professional project
and the project responsibilities you would assign
to them. what kind of training do you think they
would need to perform these responsibilities
effectively?**
<--- Score

27. What situation(s) led to this Offensive Security
Certified Professional Self Assessment?
<--- Score

28. What tools and technologies are needed for a

custom Offensive Security Certified Professional project?
<--- Score

29. Does the work address precautions for preventing penetration testers systems from being compromised?
<--- Score

30. Does our organization need more Offensive Security Certified Professional education?
<--- Score

31. What else needs to be measured?
<--- Score

32. What information do users need?
<--- Score

33. How are the Offensive Security Certified Professional's objectives aligned to the group's overall stakeholder strategy?
<--- Score

34. How does it fit into our organizational needs and tasks?
<--- Score

35. What does Offensive Security Certified Professional success mean to the stakeholders?
<--- Score

36. What would happen if Offensive Security Certified Professional weren't done?
<--- Score

37. Is account information access on a need to know basis only?
<--- Score

38. Are there any specific expectations or concerns about the Offensive Security Certified Professional team, Offensive Security Certified Professional itself?
<--- Score

39. What should be considered when identifying available resources, constraints, and deadlines?
<--- Score

40. Are there security controls that would detect or prevent testing?
<--- Score

41. Are there Offensive Security Certified Professional problems defined?
<--- Score

42. Does the tester need to provide all IP addresses from which testing will originate?
<--- Score

43. How do we Identify specific Offensive Security Certified Professional investment and emerging trends?
<--- Score

44. What training and capacity building actions are needed to implement proposed reforms?
<--- Score

45. Does your organization use a local Intrusion Prevention System(s) (IPS)?

<--- Score

46. What prevents you from making the changes you know will make you a more effective Offensive Security Certified Professional leader?
<--- Score

47. Cloud management for Offensive Security Certified Professional do we really need one?
<--- Score

48. What is the smallest subset of the problem we can usefully solve?
<--- Score

49. How do you identify the kinds of information that you will need?
<--- Score

50. Will new equipment/products be required to facilitate Offensive Security Certified Professional delivery for example is new software needed?
<--- Score

51. Anything you need to strengthen?
<--- Score

52. When a Offensive Security Certified Professional manager recognizes a problem, what options are available?
<--- Score

53. Have you identified your Offensive Security Certified Professional key performance indicators?
<--- Score

54. Is it clear when you think of the day ahead of you what activities and tasks you need to complete?
<--- Score

55. Does the penetration test agreement include client support to assist with any identified issues, mitigation strategies or vulnerability elimination steps contained in the report?
<--- Score

56. How should you recover the system if needed?
<--- Score

57. Who defines the rules in relation to any given issue?
<--- Score

58. Why do we need to keep records?
<--- Score

59. Are there recognized Offensive Security Certified Professional problems?
<--- Score

60. What are our needs in relation to Offensive Security Certified Professional skills, labor, equipment, and markets?
<--- Score

61. Is there a summary listing of items that need remediation and retesting?
<--- Score

62. Privacy violation - how much personally identifiable information could be disclosed?

<--- Score

63. How do you assess your Offensive Security Certified Professional workforce capability and capacity needs, including skills, competencies, and staffing levels?
<--- Score

64. How much are sponsors, customers, partners, stakeholders involved in Offensive Security Certified Professional? In other words, what are the risks, if Offensive Security Certified Professional does not deliver successfully?
<--- Score

Add up total points for this section:
_ _ _ _ _ = Total points for this section

Divided by: _ _ _ _ _ _ (number of statements answered) = _ _ _ _ _ _
Average score for this section

Transfer your score to the Offensive Security Certified Professional Index at the beginning of the Self-Assessment.

CRITERION #2: DEFINE:

INTENT: Formulate the stakeholder problem. Define the problem, needs and objectives.

In my belief, the answer to this question is clearly defined:

5 Strongly Agree

4 Agree

3 Neutral

2 Disagree

1 Strongly Disagree

1. What are the boundaries of the scope? What is in bounds and what is not? What is the start point? What is the stop point?
<--- Score

2. Are non-consumer users required to change password every 60 days?
<--- Score

3. Are passwords required to contain both numeric and alphabetic characters?
<--- Score

4. Is Offensive Security Certified Professional currently on schedule according to the plan?
<--- Score

5. Insecure Practices: Does the work demonstrate or teach at least one example of an insecure practice without describing how it might leave the tester or client vulnerable?
<--- Score

6. Has/have the customer(s) been identified?
<--- Score

7. Is the team adequately staffed with the desired cross-functionality? If not, what additional resources are available to the team?
<--- Score

8. How was the 'as is' process map developed, reviewed, verified and validated?
<--- Score

9. Has anyone else (internal or external to the group) attempted to solve this problem or a similar one before? If so, what knowledge can be leveraged from these previous efforts?
<--- Score

10. Are audit criteria, scope, frequency and methods defined?
<--- Score

11. Is it clearly defined in and to your organization what you do?
<--- Score

12. Is there a Offensive Security Certified Professional management charter, including stakeholder case, problem and goal statements, scope, milestones, roles and responsibilities, communication plan?
<--- Score

13. How often are the team meetings?
<--- Score

14. Has everyone on the team, including the team leaders, been properly trained?
<--- Score

15. Are roles and responsibilities formally defined?
<--- Score

16. What customer feedback methods were used to solicit their input?
<--- Score

17. In what way can we redefine the criteria of choice clients have in our category in our favor?
<--- Score

18. What are the record-keeping requirements of Offensive Security Certified Professional activities?
<--- Score

19. Do we all define Offensive Security Certified Professional in the same way?
<--- Score

20. Is there a completed SIPOC representation, describing the Suppliers, Inputs, Process, Outputs, and Customers?
<--- Score

21. How would you define the culture here?
<--- Score

22. The design must clearly define the security perimeter of the TCB. How are boundary crossings mediated?
<--- Score

23. How can the value of Offensive Security Certified Professional be defined?
<--- Score

24. What sources do you use to gather information for a Offensive Security Certified Professional study?
<--- Score

25. Is Offensive Security Certified Professional Required?
<--- Score

26. Are there different segments of customers?
<--- Score

27. Are security roles and responsibilities formally defined?
<--- Score

28. How does the Offensive Security Certified Professional manager ensure against scope creep?
<--- Score

29. Are customers identified and high impact areas defined?
<--- Score

30. Are Required Metrics Defined?
<--- Score

31. How is the team tracking and documenting its work?
<--- Score

32. Has a project plan, Gantt chart, or similar been developed/completed?
<--- Score

33. Have all basic functions of Offensive Security Certified Professional been defined?
<--- Score

34. Has a team charter been developed and communicated?
<--- Score

35. Is there regularly 100% attendance at the team meetings? If not, have appointed substitutes attended to preserve cross-functionality and full representation?
<--- Score

36. Is the type of testing clearly defined (application layer, network layer, or both)?
<--- Score

37. Will team members perform Offensive Security Certified Professional work when assigned and in a

timely fashion?
<--- Score

38. How will variation in the actual durations of each activity be dealt with to ensure that the expected Offensive Security Certified Professional results are met?
<--- Score

39. What specifically is the problem? Where does it occur? When does it occur? What is its extent?
<--- Score

40. Have specific policy objectives been defined?
<--- Score

41. Are accountability and ownership for Offensive Security Certified Professional clearly defined?
<--- Score

42. Is the attack perspective of the engagement clearly defined (internal, external, or both)?
<--- Score

43. When is/was the Offensive Security Certified Professional start date?
<--- Score

44. Is the improvement team aware of the different versions of a process: what they think it is vs. what it actually is vs. what it should be vs. what it could be?
<--- Score

45. Is data collected and displayed to better understand customer(s) critical needs and requirements.

<--- Score

46. When are meeting minutes sent out? Who is on the distribution list?
<--- Score

47. What critical content must be communicated – who, what, when, where, and how?
<--- Score

48. Are different versions of process maps needed to account for the different types of inputs?
<--- Score

49. Have all of the relationships been defined properly?
<--- Score

50. Is the team sponsored by a champion or stakeholder leader?
<--- Score

51. Is the scope of Offensive Security Certified Professional defined?
<--- Score

52. What is the minimum educational requirement for potential new hires?
<--- Score

53. Has a high-level 'as is' process map been completed, verified and validated?
<--- Score

54. Is Offensive Security Certified Professional linked to key stakeholder goals and objectives?

<--- Score

55. Have the customer needs been translated into specific, measurable requirements? How?
<--- Score

56. What would be the goal or target for a Offensive Security Certified Professional's improvement team?
<--- Score

57. Is the team formed and are team leaders (Coaches and Management Leads) assigned?
<--- Score

58. What key stakeholder process output measure(s) does Offensive Security Certified Professional leverage and how?
<--- Score

59. Skill level – what is the technical level required exploiting the vulnerability?
<--- Score

60. Is your organization subject to any specific regulatory requirements?
<--- Score

61. Are backup tapes stored in a location that does not require authorized access?
<--- Score

62. Will team members regularly document their Offensive Security Certified Professional work?
<--- Score

63. Is the current 'as is' process being followed? If not,

what are the discrepancies?
<--- Score

64. Is full participation by members in regularly held team meetings guaranteed?
<--- Score

65. Narrow or broad scope?
<--- Score

66. Is there a critical path to deliver Offensive Security Certified Professional results?
<--- Score

67. How would one define Offensive Security Certified Professional leadership?
<--- Score

68. Is the Offensive Security Certified Professional scope manageable?
<--- Score

69. What are the Roles and Responsibilities for each team member and its leadership? Where is this documented?
<--- Score

70. Is a fully trained team formed, supported, and committed to work on the Offensive Security Certified Professional improvements?
<--- Score

71. What boundaries do you define before starting a penetration test?
<--- Score

72. Is a penetration test to validate the potential exposures raised through a vulnerability assessment part of the scope of regular reviews?
<--- Score

73. Are task requirements clearly defined?
<--- Score

74. Has the Offensive Security Certified Professional work been fairly and/or equitably divided and delegated among team members who are qualified and capable to perform the work? Has everyone contributed?
<--- Score

75. How did the Offensive Security Certified Professional manager receive input to the development of a Offensive Security Certified Professional improvement plan and the estimated completion dates/times of each activity?
<--- Score

76. Are stakeholder processes mapped?
<--- Score

77. Are customer(s) identified and segmented according to their different needs and requirements?
<--- Score

78. If substitutes have been appointed, have they been briefed on the Offensive Security Certified Professional goals and received regular communications as to the progress to date?
<--- Score

79. What baselines are required to be defined and

managed?
<--- Score

80. Are there any constraints known that bear on the ability to perform Offensive Security Certified Professional work? How is the team addressing them?
<--- Score

81. Are team charters developed?
<--- Score

82. Are improvement team members fully trained on Offensive Security Certified Professional?
<--- Score

83. Do the problem and goal statements meet the SMART criteria (specific, measurable, attainable, relevant, and time-bound)?
<--- Score

84. Has the improvement team collected the 'voice of the customer' (obtained feedback – qualitative and quantitative)?
<--- Score

85. When is the estimated completion date?
<--- Score

86. What constraints exist that might impact the team?
<--- Score

87. How do you keep key subject matter experts in the loop?
<--- Score

88. Does the work address operational security during intelligence gathering phases?
<--- Score

89. How and when will the baselines be defined?
<--- Score

90. Who defines (or who defined) the rules and roles?
<--- Score

91. What are the compelling stakeholder reasons for embarking on Offensive Security Certified Professional?
<--- Score

92. What are the dynamics of the communication plan?
<--- Score

93. Is there a completed, verified, and validated high-level 'as is' (not 'should be' or 'could be') stakeholder process map?
<--- Score

94. Does the team have regular meetings?
<--- Score

95. Who are the Offensive Security Certified Professional improvement team members, including Management Leads and Coaches?
<--- Score

96. What are the rough order estimates on cost savings/opportunities that Offensive Security Certified Professional brings?
<--- Score

97. How will the Offensive Security Certified Professional team and the group measure complete success of Offensive Security Certified Professional?
<--- Score

98. What defines Best in Class?
<--- Score

99. Has the direction changed at all during the course of Offensive Security Certified Professional? If so, when did it change and why?
<--- Score

100. Are approval levels defined for contracts and supplements to contracts?
<--- Score

101. Is the team equipped with available and reliable resources?
<--- Score

102. In what way can we redefine the criteria of choice in our category in our favor, as Method introduced style and design to cleaning and Virgin America returned glamor to flying?
<--- Score

Add up total points for this section:
_____ = Total points for this section

Divided by: _____ (number of statements answered) = _____
Average score for this section

Transfer your score to the Offensive

Security Certified Professional Index at
the beginning of the Self-Assessment.

CRITERION #3: MEASURE:

INTENT: Gather the correct data.
Measure the current performance and
evolution of the situation.

In my belief, the answer to this
question is clearly defined:

5 Strongly Agree

4 Agree

3 Neutral

2 Disagree

1 Strongly Disagree

1. What has the team done to assure the stability and accuracy of the measurement process?
<--- Score

2. Who participated in the data collection for measurements?
<--- Score

3. Is it possible to estimate the impact of

**unanticipated complexity such as wrong or failed
assumptions, feedback, etc. on proposed reforms?**
<--- Score

4. Can We Measure the Return on Analysis?
<--- Score

5. What are the key input variables? What are the key
process variables? What are the key output variables?
<--- Score

6. Is this an issue for analysis or intuition?
<--- Score

7. Is there a Performance Baseline?
<--- Score

**8. When the system is attacked, what measures
or alternatives do you take to keep the system
running?**
<--- Score

9. When is Knowledge Management Measured?
<--- Score

10. How will success or failure be measured?
<--- Score

11. What evidence is there and what is measured?
<--- Score

12. Are high impact defects defined and identified in
the stakeholder process?
<--- Score

13. Is data collected on key measures that were

identified?
<--- Score

14. Is performance measured?
<--- Score

15. Why do measure/indicators matter?
<--- Score

16. Among the Offensive Security Certified Professional product and service cost to be estimated, which is considered hardest to estimate?
<--- Score

17. How Will We Measure Success?
<--- Score

18. What are my customers expectations and measures?
<--- Score

19. Does the Offensive Security Certified Professional task fit the client's priorities?
<--- Score

20. What about Offensive Security Certified Professional Analysis of results?
<--- Score

21. Have all non-recommended alternatives been analyzed in sufficient detail?
<--- Score

22. What data was collected (past, present, future/ongoing)?

<--- Score

23. How will you measure your Offensive Security Certified Professional effectiveness?
<--- Score

24. How do we know that any Offensive Security Certified Professional analysis is complete and comprehensive?
<--- Score

25. What measurements are possible, practicable and meaningful?
<--- Score

26. Is key measure data collection planned and executed, process variation displayed and communicated and performance baselined?
<--- Score

27. How frequently do we track measures?
<--- Score

28. How do we focus on what is right -not who is right?
<--- Score

29. If the operating system and application system source code cannot be reviewed, are there alternative methods to verify the proper operation of the software?
<--- Score

30. How do we do risk analysis of rare, cascading, catastrophic events?
<--- Score

31. Penetration tests are sometimes called white hat attacks because in a pen test, the good guys are attempting to break in. What are the different categories of penetration testing your organization performs?
<--- Score

32. What methods are feasible and acceptable to estimate the impact of reforms?
<--- Score

33. What will be measured?
<--- Score

34. Do staff have the necessary skills to collect, analyze, and report data?
<--- Score

35. What are the types and number of measures to use?
<--- Score

36. Which customers cant participate in our Offensive Security Certified Professional domain because they lack skills, wealth, or convenient access to existing solutions?
<--- Score

37. What potential environmental factors impact the Offensive Security Certified Professional effort?
<--- Score

38. Is the solution cost-effective?
<--- Score

39. How to measure lifecycle phases?
<--- Score

40. What doe you do if security analysis requires access to information that was sanitized?
<--- Score

41. Are we taking our company in the direction of better and revenue or cheaper and cost?
<--- Score

42. Are there measurements based on task performance?
<--- Score

43. How do you identify and analyze stakeholders and their interests?
<--- Score

44. How do your measurements capture actionable Offensive Security Certified Professional information for use in exceeding your customers expectations and securing your customers engagement?
<--- Score

45. Does Offensive Security Certified Professional analysis show the relationships among important Offensive Security Certified Professional factors?
<--- Score

46. How frequently do you track Offensive Security Certified Professional measures?
<--- Score

47. How do you measure success?
<--- Score

48. Are process variation components displayed/ communicated using suitable charts, graphs, plots?
<--- Score

49. Which customers can't participate in our market because they lack skills, wealth, or convenient access to existing solutions?
<--- Score

50. Schedule Development, Feasibility Analysis, Offensive Security Certified Professional Management, Project Closings, Technique: Using the Critical Path Method
<--- Score

51. Are the units of measure consistent?
<--- Score

52. Was a data collection plan established?
<--- Score

53. Do you utilize outside testing to verify cybersecurity effectiveness and robustness to simulated exploitation (penetration testing)?
<--- Score

54. What are our key indicators that you will measure, analyze and track?
<--- Score

55. How are you going to measure success?
<--- Score

56. How can we measure the performance?
<--- Score

57. Does Offensive Security Certified Professional analysis isolate the fundamental causes of problems?
<--- Score

58. Is Process Variation Displayed/Communicated?
<--- Score

59. Are losses documented, analyzed, and remedial processes developed to prevent future losses?
<--- Score

60. Is data collection planned and executed?
<--- Score

61. Can we do Offensive Security Certified Professional without complex (expensive) analysis?
<--- Score

62. How to measure variability?
<--- Score

63. Why do the measurements/indicators matter?
<--- Score

64. Customer Measures: How Do Customers See Us?
<--- Score

65. What are your key Offensive Security Certified Professional organizational performance measures, including key short and longer-term financial measures?

<--- Score

66. The approach of traditional Offensive Security Certified Professional works for detail complexity but is focused on a systematic approach rather than an understanding of the nature of systems themselves. what approach will permit us to deal with the kind of unpredictable emergent behaviors that dynamic complexity can introduce?
<--- Score

67. How much does downtime cost your business in regard to lost user productivity, reduced company revenue, poor customer service?
<--- Score

68. What should be measured?
<--- Score

69. Are key measures identified and agreed upon?
<--- Score

70. Does the practice systematically track and analyze outcomes related for accountability and quality improvement?
<--- Score

71. What charts has the team used to display the components of variation in the process?
<--- Score

72. How can you measure Offensive Security Certified Professional in a systematic way?
<--- Score

73. Are you taking your company in the direction of

better and revenue or cheaper and cost?
<--- Score

74. Will We Aggregate Measures across Priorities?
<--- Score

75. Have the types of risks that may impact Offensive Security Certified Professional been identified and analyzed?
<--- Score

76. Why Measure?
<--- Score

77. What is measured?
<--- Score

78. What are the uncertainties surrounding estimates of impact?
<--- Score

79. Are there any easy-to-implement alternatives to Offensive Security Certified Professional? Sometimes other solutions are available that do not require the cost implications of a full-blown project?
<--- Score

80. How is the value delivered by Offensive Security Certified Professional being measured?
<--- Score

81. Meeting the challenge: are missed Offensive Security Certified Professional opportunities costing us money?
<--- Score

82. Do we aggressively reward and promote the people who have the biggest impact on creating excellent Offensive Security Certified Professional services/products?
<--- Score

83. What are the costs of reform?
<--- Score

84. How are measurements made?
<--- Score

85. Have changes been properly/adequately analyzed for effect?
<--- Score

86. How will your organization measure success?
<--- Score

87. Does Offensive Security Certified Professional systematically track and analyze outcomes for accountability and quality improvement?
<--- Score

88. How will measures be used to manage and adapt?
<--- Score

89. How is Knowledge Management Measured?
<--- Score

90. How will effects be measured?
<--- Score

91. What Relevant Entities could be measured?
<--- Score

92. What are the agreed upon definitions of the high impact areas, defect(s), unit(s), and opportunities that will figure into the process capability metrics?
<--- Score

93. How large is the gap between current performance and the customer-specified (goal) performance?
<--- Score

94. Is a solid data collection plan established that includes measurement systems analysis?
<--- Score

95. Why should we expend time and effort to implement measurement?
<--- Score

96. What are measures?
<--- Score

97. What is the total cost related to deploying Offensive Security Certified Professional, including any consulting or professional services?
<--- Score

98. What measurements are being captured?
<--- Score

99. Which Stakeholder Characteristics Are Analyzed?
<--- Score

100. Why identify and analyze stakeholders and their interests?
<--- Score

101. Have the concerns of stakeholders to help identify and define potential barriers been obtained and analyzed?
<--- Score

102. What key measures identified indicate the performance of the stakeholder process?
<--- Score

103. Does the cost of preserving data outweigh the cost of delaying response and recovery?
<--- Score

104. What to measure and why?
<--- Score

105. Are the measurements objective?
<--- Score

106. Do we effectively measure and reward individual and team performance?
<--- Score

107. What is an unallowable cost?
<--- Score

108. What particular quality tools did the team find helpful in establishing measurements?
<--- Score

109. Is long term and short term variability accounted for?
<--- Score

110. Where is it measured?
<--- Score

111. Will Offensive Security Certified Professional have an impact on current business continuity, disaster recovery processes and/or infrastructure?
<--- Score

112. What is the right balance of time and resources between investigation, analysis, and discussion and dissemination?
<--- Score

113. Have you found any 'ground fruit' or 'low-hanging fruit' for immediate remedies to the gap in performance?
<--- Score

114. How is progress measured?
<--- Score

115. Who should receive measurement reports ?
<--- Score

Add up total points for this section:
_ _ _ _ _ = Total points for this section

Divided by: _ _ _ _ _ _ (number of statements answered) = _ _ _ _ _ _
Average score for this section

Transfer your score to the Offensive Security Certified Professional Index at the beginning of the Self-Assessment.

CRITERION #4: ANALYZE:

INTENT: Analyze causes, assumptions and hypotheses.

In my belief, the answer to this question is clearly defined:

5 Strongly Agree

4 Agree

3 Neutral

2 Disagree

1 Strongly Disagree

1. Do several people in different organizational units assist with the Offensive Security Certified Professional process?
<--- Score

2. Think about the functions involved in your Offensive Security Certified Professional project. what processes flow from these functions?
<--- Score

3. Are gaps between current performance and the goal performance identified?
<--- Score

4. What are our Offensive Security Certified Professional Processes?
<--- Score

5. Is data and process analysis, root cause analysis and quantifying the gap/opportunity in place?
<--- Score

6. What tools were used to narrow the list of possible causes?
<--- Score

7. How do you measure the Operational performance of your key work systems and processes, including productivity, cycle time, and other appropriate measures of process effectiveness, efficiency, and innovation?
<--- Score

8. What were the financial benefits resulting from any 'ground fruit or low-hanging fruit' (quick fixes)?
<--- Score

9. Is the suppliers process defined and controlled?
<--- Score

10. What are the revised rough estimates of the financial savings/opportunity for Offensive Security Certified Professional improvements?
<--- Score

11. What data is needed?

<--- Score

12. How often will data be collected for measures?
<--- Score

13. What did the team gain from developing a sub-process map?
<--- Score

14. What kind of crime could a potential new hire have committed that would not only not disqualify him/her from being hired by our organization, but would actually indicate that he/she might be a particularly good fit?
<--- Score

15. What quality tools were used to get through the analyze phase?
<--- Score

16. What are your current levels and trends in key measures or indicators of Offensive Security Certified Professional product and process performance that are important to and directly serve your customers? how do these results compare with the performance of your competitors and other organizations with similar offerings?
<--- Score

17. What process should we select for improvement?
<--- Score

18. Are critical data backed up on a daily basis?
<--- Score

19. What controls do we have in place to protect data?
<--- Score

20. Loss of confidentiality - how much data could be disclosed and how sensitive is it?
<--- Score

21. What tools were used to generate the list of possible causes?
<--- Score

22. How do mission and objectives affect the Offensive Security Certified Professional processes of our organization?
<--- Score

23. Were Pareto charts (or similar) used to portray the 'heavy hitters' (or key sources of variation)?
<--- Score

24. Did any value-added analysis or 'lean thinking' take place to identify some of the gaps shown on the 'as is' process map?
<--- Score

25. What are your current levels and trends in key Offensive Security Certified Professional measures or indicators of product and process performance that are important to and directly serve your customers?
<--- Score

26. What are the best opportunities for value improvement?
<--- Score

27. What are the disruptive Offensive Security Certified Professional technologies that enable our organization to radically change our business processes?
<--- Score

28. Loss of integrity - how much data could be corrupted and how damaging is it to the organization?
<--- Score

29. Where is the data coming from to measure compliance?
<--- Score

30. Are there documented processes and procedures in place for encryption keys?
<--- Score

31. Record-keeping requirements flow from the records needed as inputs, outputs, controls and for transformation of a Offensive Security Certified Professional process. ask yourself: are the records needed as inputs to the Offensive Security Certified Professional process available?
<--- Score

32. Do you, as a leader, bounce back quickly from setbacks?
<--- Score

33. Were any designed experiments used to generate additional insight into the data analysis?
<--- Score

34. Do our leaders quickly bounce back from

setbacks?
<--- Score

35. Have the problem and goal statements been updated to reflect the additional knowledge gained from the analyze phase?
<--- Score

36. What conclusions were drawn from the team's data collection and analysis? How did the team reach these conclusions?
<--- Score

37. If multiple processes are involved in exploiting the flaw, how does that affect classification?
<--- Score

38. Have any additional benefits been identified that will result from closing all or most of the gaps?
<--- Score

39. How do you use Offensive Security Certified Professional data and information to support organizational decision making and innovation?
<--- Score

40. Is the suppliers process defined and controlled?
<--- Score

41. What successful thing are we doing today that may be blinding us to new growth opportunities?
<--- Score

42. What are your comprehensive security safeguards for your data?

<--- Score

43. Is the Offensive Security Certified Professional process severely broken such that a re-design is necessary?
<--- Score

44. Are strong cryptography and appropriate key controls in place to safeguard data during transmission?
<--- Score

45. Are access control policies in place for data access privileges to cardholder information?
<--- Score

46. Is the performance gap determined?
<--- Score

47. What other jobs or tasks affect the performance of the steps in the Offensive Security Certified Professional process?
<--- Score

48. Was a detailed process map created to amplify critical steps of the 'as is' stakeholder process?
<--- Score

49. Did any additional data need to be collected?
<--- Score

50. Teaches and consults on quality process improvement, project management, and accelerated Offensive Security Certified Professional techniques
<--- Score

51. How do we promote understanding that opportunity for improvement is not criticism of the status quo, or the people who created the status quo?

<--- Score

52. What other organizational variables, such as reward systems or communication systems, affect the performance of this Offensive Security Certified Professional process?

<--- Score

53. Are security controls built into the application development process?

<--- Score

54. Is CVV2 or magnetic stripe data stored in the database or log files?

<--- Score

55. Qualifications of the company selected for penetration testing: what are the qualifications and backgrounds of the employees that work for the company?

<--- Score

56. Were there any improvement opportunities identified from the process analysis?

<--- Score

57. What does the data say about the performance of the stakeholder process?

<--- Score

58. How is the way you as the leader think and process information affecting your organizational culture?

<--- Score

59. Think about some of the processes you undertake within your organization. which do you own?
<--- Score

60. Was a cause-and-effect diagram used to explore the different types of causes (or sources of variation)?
<--- Score

61. When conducting a business process reengineering study, what should we look for when trying to identify business processes to change?
<--- Score

62. Are the data flows allowed only one-way from Level 4 to Level 3 and from Level 3 to Level 2?
<--- Score

63. Identify an operational issue in your organization. for example, could a particular task be done more quickly or more efficiently?
<--- Score

64. How adversely does improper modification or unauthorized changes made to your organizations data affect your organization?
<--- Score

65. Can we add value to the current Offensive Security Certified Professional decision-making process (largely qualitative) by incorporating uncertainty modeling (more quantitative)?
<--- Score

66. What are your key performance measures or indicators and in-process measures for the control and improvement of your Offensive Security Certified Professional processes?

<--- Score

67. Do your employees have the opportunity to do what they do best everyday?

<--- Score

68. What is the cost of poor quality as supported by the team's analysis?

<--- Score

69. What were the crucial 'moments of truth' on the process map?

<--- Score

70. What are our best practices for minimizing Offensive Security Certified Professional project risk, while demonstrating incremental value and quick wins throughout the Offensive Security Certified Professional project lifecycle?

<--- Score

71. An organizationally feasible system request is one that considers the mission, goals and objectives of the organization. key questions are: is the solution request practical and will it solve a problem or take advantage of an opportunity to achieve company goals?

<--- Score

72. Is externally accessible account data transmitted in unencrypted format?

<--- Score

73. How was the detailed process map generated, verified, and validated?
<--- Score

74. Client Data at Rest: Does the work consider procedures for securing client data at rest, during and/or after the engagement?
<--- Score

75. Do the data only flow from one level to other levels through a device or devices that enforce security policy between each level?
<--- Score

76. A compounding model resolution with available relevant data can often provide insight towards a solution methodology; which Offensive Security Certified Professional models, tools and techniques are necessary?
<--- Score

77. Why does a double blind penetration test provide more valuable data than a single blind test?
<--- Score

78. How does the organization define, manage, and improve its Offensive Security Certified Professional processes?
<--- Score

79. Is the gap/opportunity displayed and communicated in financial terms?
<--- Score

80. Client Data in Transit: Does the work address issues surrounding the transmission of sensitive client data between targets and penetration testers systems in the course of the engagement?
<--- Score

81. What are the qualifications and backgrounds of the employees that work for the penetration testing company?
<--- Score

82. Do all system changes go through a formal change control process?
<--- Score

Add up total points for this section:
_ _ _ _ _ = Total points for this section

Divided by: _ _ _ _ _ _ (number of statements answered) = _ _ _ _ _ _
Average score for this section

Transfer your score to the Offensive Security Certified Professional Index at the beginning of the Self-Assessment.

CRITERION #5: IMPROVE:

INTENT: Develop a practical solution. Innovate, establish and test the solution and to measure the results.

In my belief, the answer to this question is clearly defined:

5 Strongly Agree

4 Agree

3 Neutral

2 Disagree

1 Strongly Disagree

1. Who will be responsible for documenting the Offensive Security Certified Professional requirements in detail?
<--- Score

2. How does the solution remove the key sources of issues discovered in the analyze phase?
<--- Score

3. How do you improve your likelihood of success ?
<--- Score

4. How do we Improve Offensive Security Certified Professional service perception, and satisfaction?
<--- Score

5. How did the team generate the list of possible solutions?
<--- Score

6. Is a contingency plan established?
<--- Score

7. For estimation problems, how do you develop an estimation statement?
<--- Score

8. At what point will vulnerability assessments be performed once Offensive Security Certified Professional is put into production (e.g., ongoing Risk Management after implementation)?
<--- Score

9. When will another test be performed to confirm the results of the changes?
<--- Score

10. What is/are the most effective non-technical solution(s) that could be implemented in your organization to deal with malware attacks?
<--- Score

11. Is there a small-scale pilot for proposed improvement(s)? What conclusions were drawn from the outcomes of a pilot?

<--- Score

12. How do we measure improved Offensive Security Certified Professional service perception, and satisfaction?
<--- Score

13. What were the underlying assumptions on the cost-benefit analysis?
<--- Score

14. What can we do to improve?
<--- Score

15. What is the team's contingency plan for potential problems occurring in implementation?
<--- Score

16. Was a pilot designed for the proposed solution(s)?
<--- Score

17. How will you measure the results?
<--- Score

18. Is the scope clearly documented?
<--- Score

19. Is the solution technically practical?
<--- Score

20. What communications are necessary to support the implementation of the solution?
<--- Score

21. What actually has to improve and by how much?
<--- Score

22. How do you evaluate risk?
<--- Score

23. How will the team or the process owner(s) monitor the implementation plan to see that it is working as intended?
<--- Score

24. Is the implementation plan designed?
<--- Score

25. What went well, what should change, what can improve?
<--- Score

26. How will you know that you have improved?
<--- Score

27. Is the measure understandable to a variety of people?
<--- Score

28. What improvements have been achieved?
<--- Score

29. Explorations of the frontiers of Offensive Security Certified Professional will help you build influence, improve Offensive Security Certified Professional, optimize decision making, and sustain change
<--- Score

30. How does the team improve its work?
<--- Score

31. Who are the people involved in developing

and implementing Offensive Security Certified Professional?

<--- Score

32. How do you measure progress and evaluate training effectiveness?

<--- Score

33. Is pilot data collected and analyzed?

<--- Score

34. How will the group know that the solution worked?

<--- Score

35. How important is the completion of a recognized college or graduate-level degree program in the hiring decision?

<--- Score

36. Production or development system?

<--- Score

37. Is a solution implementation plan established, including schedule/work breakdown structure, resources, risk management plan, cost/budget, and control plan?

<--- Score

38. Who controls key decisions that will be made?

<--- Score

39. What is the Offensive Security Certified Professional sustainability risk?

<--- Score

40. How can we improve Offensive Security Certified Professional?
<--- Score

41. Are we Assessing Offensive Security Certified Professional and Risk?
<--- Score

42. Who will be using the results of the measurement activities?
<--- Score

43. Have you ever had system penetration testing done, and have you reviewed the results?
<--- Score

44. Is there a cost/benefit analysis of optimal solution(s)?
<--- Score

45. Do the Test cases include results of the vulnerability scans and penetration test?
<--- Score

46. For decision problems, how do you develop a decision statement?
<--- Score

47. Is Supporting Offensive Security Certified Professional documentation required?
<--- Score

48. Reputation damage - would an exploit result in reputation damage that would harm the business?
<--- Score

49. Do we combine technical expertise with business knowledge and Offensive Security Certified Professional Key topics include lifecycles, development approaches, requirements and how to make a business case?
<--- Score

50. What needs improvement?
<--- Score

51. What are the respective risks?
<--- Score

52. Why improve in the first place?
<--- Score

53. Risk events: what are the things that could go wrong?
<--- Score

54. How do we improve productivity?
<--- Score

55. How do we decide how much to remunerate an employee?
<--- Score

56. How do we go about Comparing Offensive Security Certified Professional approaches/solutions?
<--- Score

57. How significant is the improvement in the eyes of the end user?
<--- Score

58. To what extent does management recognize

Offensive Security Certified Professional as a tool to increase the results?

<--- Score

59. What is the implementation plan?

<--- Score

60. Does management take corrective action on the recommendations from the penetration test results?

<--- Score

61. What does the 'should be' process map/design look like?

<--- Score

62. Do those selected for the Offensive Security Certified Professional team have a good general understanding of what Offensive Security Certified Professional is all about?

<--- Score

63. What attendant changes will need to be made to ensure that the solution is successful?

<--- Score

64. What tools were used to evaluate the potential solutions?

<--- Score

65. What tools were most useful during the improve phase?

<--- Score

66. Risk factors: what are the characteristics of Offensive Security Certified Professional that make

it risky?
<--- Score

67. How to Improve?
<--- Score

68. Are the best solutions selected?
<--- Score

69. What tools do you use once you have decided on a Offensive Security Certified Professional strategy and more importantly how do you choose?
<--- Score

70. Is the optimal solution selected based on testing and analysis?
<--- Score

71. Were any criteria developed to assist the team in testing and evaluating potential solutions?
<--- Score

72. What are the implications of this decision 10 minutes, 10 months, and 10 years from now?
<--- Score

73. Are new and improved process ('should be') maps developed?
<--- Score

74. What do we want to improve?
<--- Score

75. Describe the design of the pilot and what tests were conducted, if any?

<--- Score

76. What is Offensive Security Certified Professional's impact on utilizing the best solution(s)?
<--- Score

77. If you could go back in time five years, what decision would you make differently? What is your best guess as to what decision you're making today you might regret five years from now?
<--- Score

78. Are we using Offensive Security Certified Professional to communicate information about our Cybersecurity Risk Management programs including the effectiveness of those programs to stakeholders, including boards, investors, auditors, and insurers?
<--- Score

79. What to do with the results or outcomes of measurements?
<--- Score

80. How do we measure risk?
<--- Score

81. How do the Offensive Security Certified Professional results compare with the performance of your competitors and other organizations with similar offerings?
<--- Score

82. Are possible solutions generated and tested?
<--- Score

83. How do we link Measurement and Risk?
<--- Score

84. How can we improve performance?
<--- Score

85. Financial damage - how much financial damage will result from an exploit?
<--- Score

86. How will the results be presented?
<--- Score

87. In the past few months, what is the smallest change we have made that has had the biggest positive result? What was it about that small change that produced the large return?
<--- Score

88. Who will be responsible for making the decisions to include or exclude requested changes once Offensive Security Certified Professional is underway?
<--- Score

89. Is there a high likelihood that any recommendations will achieve their intended results?
<--- Score

90. Does the goal represent a desired result that can be measured?
<--- Score

91. What should a proof of concept or pilot accomplish?
<--- Score

92. What is the risk?
<--- Score

93. Can the solution be designed and implemented within an acceptable time period?
<--- Score

94. What Information Is Used To Develop Penetration Tests?
<--- Score

95. What lessons, if any, from a pilot were incorporated into the design of the full-scale solution?
<--- Score

96. What error proofing will be done to address some of the discrepancies observed in the 'as is' process?
<--- Score

97. Who controls the risk?
<--- Score

98. What resources are required for the improvement effort?
<--- Score

99. What Happens To The Results Of Penetration Testing?
<--- Score

100. What can a CSP do to prepare for penetration testing and what risks are involved?
<--- Score

101. Are improved process ('should be') maps

modified based on pilot data and analysis?
<--- Score

102. What is the magnitude of the improvements?
<--- Score

103. Does a firm engaged to perform a penetration test present management with a written report documenting the results of the test?
<--- Score

104. How do you manage and improve your Offensive Security Certified Professional work systems to deliver customer value and achieve organizational success and sustainability?
<--- Score

105. How are evaluators to judge the security of a system composed of individually evaluated components?
<--- Score

106. How can skill-level changes improve Offensive Security Certified Professional?
<--- Score

107. Does the firm engaged to perform the penetration test present management with a written report documenting the results of the test?
<--- Score

108. How will you know when its improved?
<--- Score

109. What is/are the most effective technical solution(s) that are implemented at the network

level to deal with malware attacks?

<--- Score

110. Are there any constraints (technical, political, cultural, or otherwise) that would inhibit certain solutions?

<--- Score

111. What are the risks and constraints that you should be concerned about?

<--- Score

112. Have you implemented a holistic approach to vendor risk management?

<--- Score

113. What tools were used to tap into the creativity and encourage 'outside the box' thinking?

<--- Score

114. What actually has to improve and by how much?

<--- Score

115. How do you decide which supplier to choose?

<--- Score

116. How do we keep improving Offensive Security Certified Professional?

<--- Score

117. How will we know that a change is improvement?

<--- Score

118. Do we cover the five essential competencies-Communication, Collaboration,Innovation,

Adaptability, and Leadership that improve an organization's ability to leverage the new Offensive Security Certified Professional in a volatile global economy?
<--- Score

Add up total points for this section:
_____ = Total points for this section

Divided by: _____ (number of statements answered) = _____
Average score for this section

Transfer your score to the Offensive Security Certified Professional Index at the beginning of the Self-Assessment.

CRITERION #6: CONTROL:

INTENT: Implement the practical solution. Maintain the performance and correct possible complications.

In my belief, the answer to this question is clearly defined:

5 Strongly Agree

4 Agree

3 Neutral

2 Disagree

1 Strongly Disagree

1. Can Offensive Security Certified Professional be learned?
<--- Score

2. How will the process owner and team be able to hold the gains?
<--- Score

3. Do you have plans or processes to protect your

companys important assets, Information?
<--- Score

4. Who has control over resources?
<--- Score

5. Is a security incident response plan formally documented?
<--- Score

6. What are the known security controls?
<--- Score

7. What should the next improvement project be that is related to Offensive Security Certified Professional?
<--- Score

8. What is the control/monitoring plan?
<--- Score

9. Does the response plan contain a definite closed loop continual improvement scheme (e.g., plan-do-check-act)?
<--- Score

10. Who is the Offensive Security Certified Professional process owner?
<--- Score

11. Are operating procedures consistent?
<--- Score

12. Will any special training be provided for results interpretation?
<--- Score

13. Are security alerts from the intrusion detection sensor monitored 24 hours a day, 7 days a week?
<--- Score

14. Is a response plan established and deployed?
<--- Score

15. Implementation Planning- is a pilot needed to test the changes before a full roll out occurs?
<--- Score

16. Are the disaster recovery plan (DRP) and the business contingency plan (BCP) tested annually?
<--- Score

17. Is there a control plan in place for sustaining improvements (short and long-term)?
<--- Score

18. What Enterprise Resource Planning (ERP) application(s) does your organization use?
<--- Score

19. Are pertinent alerts monitored, analyzed and distributed to appropriate personnel?
<--- Score

20. What is your theory of human motivation, and how does your compensation plan fit with that view?
<--- Score

21. How do you encourage people to take control and responsibility?
<--- Score

22. A key requirement for the penetration test plan

is defining the posture of the simulated attacker. Is the evaluator to play the role of an insider or an external unauthorized user?
<--- Score

23. What are your results for key measures or indicators of the accomplishment of your Offensive Security Certified Professional strategy and action plans, including building and strengthening core competencies?
<--- Score

24. What are we attempting to measure/monitor?
<--- Score

25. How might the group capture best practices and lessons learned so as to leverage improvements?
<--- Score

26. Whats the best design framework for Offensive Security Certified Professional organization now that, in a post industrial-age if the top-down, command and control model is no longer relevant?
<--- Score

27. How will report readings be checked to effectively monitor performance?
<--- Score

28. How will new or emerging customer needs/ requirements be checked/communicated to orient the process toward meeting the new specifications and continually reducing variation?
<--- Score

29. Have new or revised work instructions resulted?

<--- Score

30. Has the penetration tester performed assessments against organizations of similar size and scope?
<--- Score

31. How will the process owner verify improvement in present and future sigma levels, process capabilities?
<--- Score

32. Were the planned controls in place?
<--- Score

33. Is there a standardized process?
<--- Score

34. Is there documentation that will support the successful operation of the improvement?
<--- Score

35. Is knowledge gained on process shared and institutionalized?
<--- Score

36. How will input, process, and output variables be checked to detect for sub-optimal conditions?
<--- Score

37. What do we stand for--and what are we against?
<--- Score

38. What are the critical parameters to watch?
<--- Score

39. In the case of a Offensive Security Certified Professional project, the criteria for the audit derive from implementation objectives. an audit of a Offensive Security Certified Professional project involves assessing whether the recommendations outlined for implementation have been met. Can we track that any Offensive Security Certified Professional project is implemented as planned, and is it working?
<--- Score

40. Do the decisions we make today help people and the planet tomorrow?
<--- Score

41. How can we best use all of our knowledge repositories to enhance learning and sharing?
<--- Score

42. Who controls critical resources?
<--- Score

43. Is new knowledge gained imbedded in the response plan?
<--- Score

44. What other systems, operations, processes, and infrastructures (hiring practices, staffing, training, incentives/rewards, metrics/dashboards/scorecards, etc.) need updates, additions, changes, or deletions in order to facilitate knowledge transfer and improvements?
<--- Score

45. Are there industry-standard penetration testing certifications held by the penetration

tester?
<--- Score

46. Does Offensive Security Certified Professional appropriately measure and monitor risk?
<--- Score

47. Is a response plan in place for when the input, process, or output measures indicate an 'out-of-control' condition?
<--- Score

48. Does a troubleshooting guide exist or is it needed?
<--- Score

49. If penetration testing has been determined to be reasonable and appropriate, has specifically worded, written approval from senior management been received for any planned penetration testing?
<--- Score

50. Do you monitor the effectiveness of your Offensive Security Certified Professional activities?
<--- Score

51. Are the version control and configuration management policies consistent throughout the organization for all applications?
<--- Score

52. What should we measure to verify efficiency gains?
<--- Score

53. Has the improved process and its steps been

standardized?
<--- Score

54. Where do ideas that reach policy makers and planners as proposals for Offensive Security Certified Professional strengthening and reform actually originate?
<--- Score

55. What are the key elements of your Offensive Security Certified Professional performance improvement system, including your evaluation, organizational learning, and innovation processes?
<--- Score

56. Do the Offensive Security Certified Professional decisions we make today help people and the planet tomorrow?
<--- Score

57. What is the recommended frequency of auditing?
<--- Score

58. Are pertinent security alerts monitored, analyzed and distributed to appropriate personnel?
<--- Score

59. What are the reporting expectations for the penetration test plan?
<--- Score

60. Does job training on the documented procedures need to be part of the process team's education and training?

<--- Score

61. Who sets the Offensive Security Certified Professional standards?
<--- Score

62. Is your firewall and router configured to conform with documented security standards?
<--- Score

63. Is there a Offensive Security Certified Professional Communication plan covering who needs to get what information when?
<--- Score

64. Are operational controls effective?
<--- Score

65. Is there a documented and implemented monitoring plan?
<--- Score

66. What quality tools were useful in the control phase?
<--- Score

67. Is your firewalls CPU utilization monitored at least every 15 minutes?
<--- Score

68. How do our controls stack up?
<--- Score

69. What can you control?
<--- Score

70. Are documented procedures clear and easy to follow for the operators?
<--- Score

71. Do the tools used for the penetration test need to be listed anywhere else besides in the Penetration Test Plan document?
<--- Score

72. Is reporting being used or needed?
<--- Score

73. Do we monitor the Offensive Security Certified Professional decisions made and fine tune them as they evolve?
<--- Score

74. Does the Offensive Security Certified Professional performance meet the customer's requirements?
<--- Score

75. How do you select, collect, align, and integrate Offensive Security Certified Professional data and information for tracking daily operations and overall organizational performance, including progress relative to strategic objectives and action plans?
<--- Score

76. What key inputs and outputs are being measured on an ongoing basis?
<--- Score

77. Who will be in control?
<--- Score

78. Potential Threats: Does the work address issues with conducting tests against systems over hostile networks, such as the public Internet or unencrypted wireless?
<--- Score

79. Is there a transfer of ownership and knowledge to process owner and process team tasked with the responsibilities.
<--- Score

80. Measure, Monitor and Predict Offensive Security Certified Professional Activities to Optimize Operations and Profitably, and Enhance Outcomes
<--- Score

81. Are only crypto devices used that meet the approval standards and policies of your organization?
<--- Score

82. Is there a recommended audit plan for routine surveillance inspections of Offensive Security Certified Professional's gains?
<--- Score

83. Are new process steps, standards, and documentation ingrained into normal operations?
<--- Score

84. How will the day-to-day responsibilities for monitoring and continual improvement be transferred from the improvement team to the process owner?
<--- Score

85. Are suggested corrective/restorative actions indicated on the response plan for known causes to problems that might surface?
<--- Score

86. What should we measure to verify effectiveness gains?
<--- Score

87. Is access to the data center restricted and closely monitored?
<--- Score

88. Against what alternative is success being measured?
<--- Score

89. Are there documented procedures?
<--- Score

90. Were the planned controls working?
<--- Score

91. How likely is the current Offensive Security Certified Professional plan to come in on schedule or on budget?
<--- Score

92. What are you trying to protect against?
<--- Score

93. Why is change control necessary?
<--- Score

94. What is our theory of human motivation, and how does our compensation plan fit with that

view?
<--- Score

95. How do controls support value?
<--- Score

96. Will existing staff require re-training, for example, to learn new business processes?
<--- Score

97. What other areas of the group might benefit from the Offensive Security Certified Professional team's improvements, knowledge, and learning?
<--- Score

98. Are controls in place and consistently applied?
<--- Score

Add up total points for this section:
_ _ _ _ _ = Total points for this section

Divided by: _ _ _ _ _ _ (number of statements answered) = _ _ _ _ _ _
Average score for this section

Transfer your score to the Offensive Security Certified Professional Index at the beginning of the Self-Assessment.

CRITERION #7: SUSTAIN:

INTENT: Retain the benefits.

In my belief, the answer to this
question is clearly defined:

5 Strongly Agree

4 Agree

3 Neutral

2 Disagree

1 Strongly Disagree

**1. How do we provide a safe environment
-physically and emotionally?**
<--- Score

**2. Would you prefer the Information Security
Office to perform a network-based assessment?**
<--- Score

3. Instead of going to current contacts for new ideas,
what if you reconnected with dormant contacts--
the people you used to know? If you were going

reactivate a dormant tie, who would it be?
<--- Score

4. Any new, unexpected members in admin groups?
<--- Score

5. How will we know if we have been successful?
<--- Score

6. Why would you end your test before the allotted time-frame?
<--- Score

7. What are the pros and cons of doing vulnerability scanning and penetration testing remotely vs onsite?
<--- Score

8. Do you review audit logs at least once a week on critical systems?
<--- Score

9. How many years experience does the penetration tester have?
<--- Score

10. What are the long-term Offensive Security Certified Professional goals?
<--- Score

11. What one word do we want to own in the minds of our customers, employees, and partners?
<--- Score

12. What are the top 3 things at the forefront

of our Offensive Security Certified Professional agendas for the next 3 years?
<--- Score

13. Are there any disadvantages to implementing Offensive Security Certified Professional? There might be some that are less obvious?
<--- Score

14. What may be the consequences for the performance of an organization if all stakeholders are not consulted regarding Offensive Security Certified Professional?
<--- Score

15. What are all of our Offensive Security Certified Professional domains and what do they do?
<--- Score

16. How important is Offensive Security Certified Professional to the user organizations mission?
<--- Score

17. What criteria does your organization use to determine the competence of an internal and/or third-party penetration tester and/or auditors?
<--- Score

18. Do you know what you are doing? And who do you call if you don't?
<--- Score

19. How do we accomplish our long range Offensive Security Certified Professional goals?
<--- Score

20. What can you defend?
<--- Score

21. Is our strategy driving our strategy? Or is the way in which we allocate resources driving our strategy?
<--- Score

22. White Box or Black Box?
<--- Score

23. How do we keep the momentum going?
<--- Score

24. What is our question?
<--- Score

25. Schedule -can it be done in the given time?
<--- Score

26. Do you or any third parties conduct any penetration & vulnerability testing?
<--- Score

27. Do you perform background checks?
<--- Score

28. What are you trying to protect?
<--- Score

29. Which Offensive Security Certified Professional goals are the most important?
<--- Score

30. How likely is it that a customer would recommend our company to a friend or colleague?
<--- Score

31. Are security patches tested before they are deployed to production systems?
<--- Score

32. Who Is Responsible For Penetration Testing?
<--- Score

33. Are group passwords allowed on critical systems?
<--- Score

34. If penetration testing is performed after acceptance testing and security flaws are found, is the vendor obligated to fix the flaws?
<--- Score

35. Are interfaces to the system in proper state and configuration?
<--- Score

36. What trophy do we want on our mantle?
<--- Score

37. Are we changing as fast as the world around us?
<--- Score

38. Will it be accepted by users?
<--- Score

39. If you were responsible for initiating and implementing major changes in your organization, what steps might you take to ensure acceptance of those changes?
<--- Score

40. How are we doing compared to our industry?
<--- Score

41. What is the disadvantage of letting the companys employees know about the penetration test?
<--- Score

42. What are the rules and assumptions my industry operates under? What if the opposite were true?
<--- Score

43. What areas of the code does the penetration tests hit?
<--- Score

44. Motive - how motivated is a group of attackers to find and exploit a vulnerability?
<--- Score

45. Does your organization do background checks on new hires?
<--- Score

46. How do we foster the skills, knowledge, talents, attributes, and characteristics we want to have?
<--- Score

47. Do the operating system and application system executable codes match expected profiles?
<--- Score

48. What are your most important goals for the strategic Offensive Security Certified Professional objectives?

<--- Score

49. Intrusion detection - how likely is an exploit to be detected?
<--- Score

50. What are internal and external Offensive Security Certified Professional relations?
<--- Score

51. What are the compelling reasons to perform a penetration test?
<--- Score

52. What will the initial level of access and the amount of information be?
<--- Score

53. What can go wrong?
<--- Score

54. Where are your backups?
<--- Score

55. What are the basics of Offensive Security Certified Professional fraud?
<--- Score

56. What stupid rule would we most like to kill?
<--- Score

57. How is the configuration management policy enforced?
<--- Score

58. Is the impact that Offensive Security Certified

Professional has shown?

<--- Score

59. Will you violate an SLA?

<--- Score

60. Are all employees subject to background and criminal history checks before they are granted access?

<--- Score

61. What systems/resources will be initially tested and how?

<--- Score

62. Are individuals allowed to submit a new password that is the same as a previous password?

<--- Score

63. Non-compliance - how much exposure does non-compliance introduce?

<--- Score

64. Do we have past Offensive Security Certified Professional Successes?

<--- Score

65. What is our competitive advantage?

<--- Score

66. Has the software undergone any penetration testing?

<--- Score

67. What will happen if your organization has a breach?

<--- Score

68. Are we making progress? and are we making progress as Offensive Security Certified Professional leaders?
<--- Score

69. Is this project beneficial to your study of application software security?
<--- Score

70. What new services of functionality will be implemented next with Offensive Security Certified Professional ?
<--- Score

71. Do we think we know, or do we know we know ?
<--- Score

72. Are we paying enough attention to the partners our company depends on to succeed?
<--- Score

73. How do we engage the workforce, in addition to satisfying them?
<--- Score

74. Is there any existing Offensive Security Certified Professional governance structure?
<--- Score

75. What potential megatrends could make our business model obsolete?
<--- Score

76. How many Internet-facing hosts do you want the Information Security Office to assess?
<--- Score

77. Who is going to care?
<--- Score

78. Would you prefer the Information Security Office to perform an application security assessment?
<--- Score

79. Is there a security awareness and training program in place?
<--- Score

80. Are anti-virus/anti-malware signatures up to date?
<--- Score

81. Under Attack: Can your systems really benefit from penetration testing?
<--- Score

82. Do you keep 50% of your time unscheduled?
<--- Score

83. How do we foster innovation?
<--- Score

84. Does your organization perform penetration testing of all Internet-facing applications?
<--- Score

85. How to Secure Offensive Security Certified Professional?

<--- Score

86. We picked a method, now what?
<--- Score

87. What Is a Nonintrusive Attack?
<--- Score

88. What must you defend?
<--- Score

89. How do you use coloured Petri nets to model penetration testing attacks?
<--- Score

90. Is patching up to date?
<--- Score

91. Who is On the Team?
<--- Score

92. What is our formula for success in Offensive Security Certified Professional ?
<--- Score

93. At what moment would you think; Will I get fired?
<--- Score

94. Are new systems, as delivered and installed, in a state consistent with its expected design and operation?
<--- Score

95. How does Offensive Security Certified Professional integrate with other stakeholder initiatives?

<--- Score

96. What will be used to confirm that unauthorized access was obtained?
<--- Score

97. What Information Can Be Obtained by Port Scanning?
<--- Score

98. Are non-consumer user accounts locked within 6 invalid login attempts?
<--- Score

99. Big-Bang or Continuous?
<--- Score

100. What is our Offensive Security Certified Professional Strategy?
<--- Score

101. What happens when a new employee joins the organization?
<--- Score

102. Are password protected screen savers or terminal locks used on all critical systems?
<--- Score

103. Are applications run on default installations of operating systems?
<--- Score

104. Design Thinking: Integrating Innovation, Offensive Security Certified Professional, and Brand Value

<--- Score

105. If all the other components are rated (previously penetration tested), is the whole retested, or just the new component, its interfaces, and its environment assumptions?
<--- Score

106. Is more than one application running as the primary function of a server at any given time?
<--- Score

107. Do you perform penetration testing on your network and applications at least once a year and after any significant modifications?
<--- Score

108. Do you have an implicit bias for capital investments over people investments?
<--- Score

109. Any unauthorized physical access?
<--- Score

110. Ease of exploit - how easy is it for a group of attackers to actually exploit a vulnerability?
<--- Score

111. Are you failing differently each time?
<--- Score

112. Why should we adopt a Offensive Security Certified Professional framework?
<--- Score

113. Have anti-virus signature files been updated

to the latest signature file?
<--- Score

114. What Information Can Be Collected About Network Hosts?
<--- Score

115. How often does penetration testing of Internet-facing applications occur?
<--- Score

116. What will drive Offensive Security Certified Professional change?
<--- Score

117. Are you a specific target?
<--- Score

118. How do you trace those who attacked your organization?
<--- Score

119. What management system can we use to leverage the Offensive Security Certified Professional experience, ideas, and concerns of the people closest to the work to be done?
<--- Score

120. Who uses our product in ways we never expected?
<--- Score

121. What is the funding source for this project?
<--- Score

122. What are the Key enablers to make this

Offensive Security Certified Professional move?
<--- Score

123. What are the usability implications of Offensive Security Certified Professional actions?
<--- Score

124. Is there a limit on the number of users in Offensive Security Certified Professional ?
<--- Score

125. What is it like to work for me?
<--- Score

126. What happens at this company when people fail?
<--- Score

127. Must new employees or contractor employees pass several tests and background checks before they are allowed unescorted access to protected areas?
<--- Score

128. Ease of discoverability - how easy is it for a group of attackers to discover a vulnerability in your organization?
<--- Score

129. Operational - will it work?
<--- Score

130. What business benefits will Offensive Security Certified Professional goals deliver if achieved?
<--- Score

131. What does your signature ensure?

<--- Score

132. How long will it take to change?
<--- Score

133. Whom among your colleagues do you trust, and for what?
<--- Score

134. Which specific applications?
<--- Score

135. What are the different categories of penetration testing?
<--- Score

136. Are audit logs retained for at least six months on all critical systems?
<--- Score

137. How many employees use remote access services?
<--- Score

138. Why is it important to have senior management support for a Offensive Security Certified Professional project?
<--- Score

139. Who should conduct the test?
<--- Score

140. Are there Offensive Security Certified Professional Models?
<--- Score

141. What would have to be true for the option on the table to be the best possible choice?
<--- Score

142. How will we build a 100-year startup?
<--- Score

143. How do you stay inspired?
<--- Score

144. What assets are you trying to protect?
<--- Score

145. How do we manage Offensive Security Certified Professional Knowledge Management (KM)?
<--- Score

146. How can we incorporate support to ensure safe and effective use of Offensive Security Certified Professional into the services that we provide?
<--- Score

147. What threat is Offensive Security Certified Professional addressing?
<--- Score

148. Among our stronger employees, how many see themselves at the company in three years? How many would leave for a 10 percent raise from another company?
<--- Score

149. What was the last experiment we ran?
<--- Score

150. Which individuals, teams or departments will be involved in Offensive Security Certified Professional?
<--- Score

151. What is the overall business strategy?
<--- Score

152. Which systems are compromised?
<--- Score

153. What current systems have to be understood and/or changed?
<--- Score

154. Where is our petri dish?
<--- Score

155. If you had to rebuild your organization without any traditional competitive advantages (i.e., no killer a technology, promising research, innovative product/service delivery model, etc.), how would your people have to approach their work and collaborate together in order to create the necessary conditions for success?
<--- Score

156. If you had to leave your organization for a year and the only communication you could have with employees was a single paragraph, what would you write?
<--- Score

157. Is rapid recovery the most important thing for you?
<--- Score

158. What type of authentication do you use for your web services?

<--- Score

159. Are all unnecessary services disabled on a server?

<--- Score

160. What did we miss in the interview for the worst hire we ever made?

<--- Score

161. Which models, tools and techniques are necessary?

<--- Score

162. Is it top secret?

<--- Score

163. What are current Offensive Security Certified Professional Paradigms?

<--- Score

164. How vulnerable is the network, host, and application(s) to attacks from the internet or intranet?

<--- Score

165. Are you satisfied with your current role? If not, what is missing from it?

<--- Score

166. Are CDAs associated with safety allocated to Level 4 and protected from all lower levels?

<--- Score

167. Do you perform penetration testing of the service?
<--- Score

168. What will be the consequences to the stakeholder (financial, reputation etc) if Offensive Security Certified Professional does not go ahead or fails to deliver the objectives?
<--- Score

169. How do we ensure that implementations of Offensive Security Certified Professional products are done in a way that ensures safety?
<--- Score

170. Has your organization performed a penetration test in the last year?
<--- Score

171. Are modems connected to the internal systems?
<--- Score

172. Has the product undergone any penetration testing?
<--- Score

173. If our company went out of business tomorrow, would anyone who doesn't get a paycheck here care?
<--- Score

174. Who are you going to put out of business, and why?
<--- Score

175. How often does a utility engage with an independent third-party to engage in penetration testing of networks, such as AMI, operations, other mainframes, etc.?
<--- Score

176. Is firewall administration limited to only the network security administration staff?
<--- Score

177. Does the system function properly within its entire range of design parameters?
<--- Score

178. Is Offensive Security Certified Professional realistic, or are you setting yourself up for failure?
<--- Score

179. In what ways are Offensive Security Certified Professional vendors and us interacting to ensure safe and effective use?
<--- Score

180. What is the purpose of Offensive Security Certified Professional in relation to the mission?
<--- Score

181. If your customer were your grandmother, would you tell her to buy what we're selling?
<--- Score

182. If no one would ever find out about your accomplishments, how would you lead differently?
<--- Score

183. Have all applications undergone penetration

testing?

<--- Score

184. Are unnecessary services running?

<--- Score

185. What are the Essentials of Internal Offensive Security Certified Professional Management?

<--- Score

186. Would you prefer the Information Security Office to perform a host-based assessment?

<--- Score

187. Is it tested with or without administrative credentials?

<--- Score

188. Can an intruder obtain unauthorized access to critical resources?

<--- Score

189. How will you contain it?

<--- Score

190. Does the asset or system directly perform the safety function?

<--- Score

191. Who is responsible for ensuring appropriate resources (time, people and money) are allocated to Offensive Security Certified Professional?

<--- Score

192. When should you inform the authorities?

<--- Score

193. What do we do when new problems arise?
<--- Score

194. Does your organization have any systems that use modems?
<--- Score

195. What do you audit?
<--- Score

196. Are all media devices properly inventoried and securely stored?
<--- Score

197. How will we insure seamless interoperability of Offensive Security Certified Professional moving forward?
<--- Score

198. Have new benefits been realized?
<--- Score

199. Why is Offensive Security Certified Professional important for you now?
<--- Score

200. Have benefits been optimized with all key stakeholders?
<--- Score

201. Who, on the executive team or the board, has spoken to a customer recently?
<--- Score

202. How can we become the company that would

put us out of business?
<--- Score

203. What is the range of capabilities?
<--- Score

204. Why should people listen to you?
<--- Score

205. Do we have the right people on the bus?
<--- Score

206. Think about the kind of project structure that would be appropriate for your Offensive Security Certified Professional project. should it be formal and complex, or can it be less formal and relatively simple?
<--- Score

207. How do we make it meaningful in connecting Offensive Security Certified Professional with what users do day-to-day?
<--- Score

208. What is Effective Offensive Security Certified Professional?
<--- Score

209. What is the disadvantage of letting the IT staff know about the penetration test?
<--- Score

210. Is scanning for vulnerabilities legal?
<--- Score

211. How do you determine the key elements that

affect Offensive Security Certified Professional workforce satisfaction? how are these elements determined for different workforce groups and segments?

<--- Score

212. You may have created your customer policies at a time when you lacked resources, technology wasn't up-to-snuff, or low service levels were the industry norm. Have those circumstances changed?

<--- Score

213. Is confidential account information transmitted via unencrypted email format?

<--- Score

214. How much does Offensive Security Certified Professional help?

<--- Score

215. What are the barriers to increased Offensive Security Certified Professional production?

<--- Score

216. Does your organization obtain penetration tests and regular security scans of the network?

<--- Score

217. Who will determine interim and final deadlines?

<--- Score

218. What is the estimated value of the project?

<--- Score

219. Does the asset or system have any network connections with any other systems at the same security level?
<--- Score

220. Do Offensive Security Certified Professional rules make a reasonable demand on a users capabilities?
<--- Score

221. What are specific Offensive Security Certified Professional Rules to follow?
<--- Score

222. How can we become more high-tech but still be high touch?
<--- Score

223. Awareness - how well known is a vulnerability to a group of attackers?
<--- Score

224. What is the difference between penetration testing and hacking/intrusion?
<--- Score

225. Who will provide the final approval of Offensive Security Certified Professional deliverables?
<--- Score

226. Does a review of the operating system and application system source code reveal unacceptable deficiencies, vulnerabilities, design flaws, or lack of robustness?
<--- Score

227. Are all internal and external dormant

accounts removed?

<--- Score

228. What is something you believe that nearly no one agrees with you on?

<--- Score

229. What happens if you do not have enough funding?

<--- Score

230. Does your organization use site-to-site Virtual Private Network (VPN) tunnels?

<--- Score

231. Who is the main stakeholder, with ultimate responsibility for driving Offensive Security Certified Professional forward?

<--- Score

232. How can you negotiate Offensive Security Certified Professional successfully with a stubborn boss, an irate client, or a deceitful coworker?

<--- Score

233. What counts that we are not counting?

<--- Score

234. In retrospect, of the projects that we pulled the plug on, what percent do we wish had been allowed to keep going, and what percent do we wish had ended earlier?

<--- Score

235. How to deal with Offensive Security Certified Professional Changes?

<--- Score

236. How do you keep evidence for possible legal action?
<--- Score

237. What have we done to protect our business from competitive encroachment?
<--- Score

238. Whose voice (department, ethnic group, women, older workers, etc) might you have missed hearing from in your company, and how might you amplify this voice to create positive momentum for your business?
<--- Score

239. Are firewalls used internally to separate networks of different security levels?
<--- Score

240. How do we Lead with Offensive Security Certified Professional in Mind?
<--- Score

241. What are strategies for increasing support and reducing opposition?
<--- Score

242. Is there a clear consideration of the automated and manual testing that was performed?
<--- Score

243. Has an attack and penetration test ever been performed by staff (such as the internal auditor)?

<--- Score

244. Does your organization use a local Firewall(s)?
<--- Score

245. Is a Offensive Security Certified Professional Team Work effort in place?
<--- Score

246. Do you perform Automated Vulnerability Scanning?
<--- Score

247. If we do not follow, then how to lead?
<--- Score

248. Is there any limitation to the hours in which scanning penetration testing can be performed?
<--- Score

249. Where do you see the most significant contribution/justification for the existence of the hacker community?
<--- Score

250. Is access to keys restricted to the fewest number of custodians necessary?
<--- Score

251. Is maximizing Offensive Security Certified Professional protection the same as minimizing Offensive Security Certified Professional loss?
<--- Score

252. How is the security officer/administrator authenticated?

<--- Score

253. What services do you expose to the internet?
<--- Score

254. Would you consider integrating yourself in the owasp community and contributing to it in near future?
<--- Score

255. How do we maintain Offensive Security Certified Professional's Integrity?
<--- Score

256. How do we know if we are successful?
<--- Score

257. Do we have enough freaky customers in our portfolio pushing us to the limit day in and day out?
<--- Score

258. Do you see more potential in people than they do in themselves?
<--- Score

259. Is a vulnerability scan or penetration test performed on all internet-facing applications and systems before they go into production?
<--- Score

260. What is considered evidence?
<--- Score

261. Does the organization want updates regarding ongoing exploitation of systems during the test?

<--- Score

262. Are penetration tests conducted on a regularly scheduled basis as well as whenever significant changes have occurred within the organizations network?
<--- Score

263. Which criteria are used to determine which projects are going to be pursued or discarded?
<--- Score

264. Does the organization perform any penetration testing for its mission critical systems?
<--- Score

265. In a project to restructure Offensive Security Certified Professional outcomes, which stakeholders would you involve?
<--- Score

266. Are available security patches implemented within 30 days?
<--- Score

267. Are file comparison checks being reviewed on critical systems at least once a day?
<--- Score

268. Who are four people whose careers I've enhanced?
<--- Score

269. Who do we want our customers to become?
<--- Score

270. How do we go about Securing Offensive Security Certified Professional?
<--- Score

271. Are you going to do physical penetrations?
<--- Score

272. What trouble can we get into?
<--- Score

273. What should we stop doing?
<--- Score

274. What information is critical to our organization that our executives are ignoring?
<--- Score

275. Loss of availability - how much service could be lost and how vital is it?
<--- Score

276. How do senior leaders deploy your organizations vision and values through your leadership system, to the workforce, to key suppliers and partners, and to customers and other stakeholders, as appropriate?
<--- Score

277. What is the craziest thing we can do?
<--- Score

278. Do logs include date and time stamp on all critical systems?
<--- Score

279. Has an attack and penetration test ever been

performed by an external party?
<--- Score

280. If we got kicked out and the board brought in a new CEO, what would he do?
<--- Score

281. How fast should the network typically respond?
<--- Score

282. Who are the key stakeholders?
<--- Score

283. Is the Offensive Security Certified Professional organization completing tasks effectively and efficiently?
<--- Score

284. Is it economical; do we have the time and money?
<--- Score

285. What is the time interval for the test?
<--- Score

286. Why are physical penetration and operations penetration tests valuable to system security?
<--- Score

287. Why are Offensive Security Certified Professional skills important?
<--- Score

288. Who do we think the world wants us to be?
<--- Score

289. Who are your service providers?
<--- Score

290. Are actions related to encryption key management logged on all servers that utilize the keys?
<--- Score

291. Any gaps in logs?
<--- Score

292. Where is the threat?
<--- Score

293. Is there any limitation to the hours in which scanning / penetration testing can be performed?
<--- Score

294. If we weren't already in this business, would we enter it today? And if not, what are we going to do about it?
<--- Score

295. What is likely to be attacked?
<--- Score

296. Does your organization use any Remote Access services?
<--- Score

297. What antivirus application(s) do you use?
<--- Score

298. Are the latest intrusion detection system (IDS) signatures installed on all IDS sensors?

<--- Score

299. In the past year, what have you done (or could you have done) to increase the accurate perception of this company/brand as ethical and honest?
<--- Score

300. Are all passwords on network devices and systems encrypted?
<--- Score

301. What are the gaps in my knowledge and experience?
<--- Score

302. Would you rather sell to knowledgeable and informed customers or to uninformed customers?
<--- Score

303. How does a penetration test differ from a vulnerability scan?
<--- Score

304. What information will a threat model help to provide?
<--- Score

305. Who will be responsible for deciding whether Offensive Security Certified Professional goes ahead or not after the initial investigations?
<--- Score

306. Who else should we help?
<--- Score

307. What are the success criteria that will indicate

that Offensive Security Certified Professional objectives have been met and the benefits delivered?
<--- Score

308. What kind of public notification?
<--- Score

309. How do we create Buy-in?
<--- Score

310. What vulnerabilities might your organizations assets have?
<--- Score

311. Design Thinking: Integrating Innovation, Offensive Security Certified Professional Experience, and Brand Value
<--- Score

312. Who will be notified of the test?
<--- Score

313. What role does communication play in the success or failure of a Offensive Security Certified Professional project?
<--- Score

314. What would you recommend your friend do if he/she were facing this dilemma?
<--- Score

315. What should be tested?
<--- Score

316. Does your organization use a local Intrusion Detection System(s) (IDS)?

<--- Score

317. How do you make it systematic?
<--- Score

318. What would you recommend doing in order make it impossible for outsiders to (a) successfully test internal hosts connectivity, and (b) map your organizations network?
<--- Score

319. What is your BATNA (best alternative to a negotiated agreement)?
<--- Score

320. Is the use of NAT or PAT implemented into your environment to hide the internal network from the Internet?
<--- Score

321. Do you unplug or not?
<--- Score

322. Does the work address precautions for maintaining the security of client systems during the test?
<--- Score

323. Who should pay for it?
<--- Score

324. Who Uses What?
<--- Score

325. What knowledge, skills and characteristics mark a good Offensive Security Certified

Professional project manager?
<--- Score

326. Any unauthorized hardware suddenly appearing?
<--- Score

327. How likely are those threats to materialize?
<--- Score

328. Where do Attackers get the Most Traction?
<--- Score

329. Is application penetration testing used to simulate internal hacking situations?
<--- Score

330. To whom do you add value?
<--- Score

331. Is it preferred that the Information Security Office performs compliance, physical or enterprise assessments?
<--- Score

332. Is there a formal procedure for approving all external connections?
<--- Score

333. Where can we break convention?
<--- Score

334. Why don't our customers like us?
<--- Score

335. Do you have any supplemental information to

add to this checklist?
<--- Score

336. When performing automated vulnerability and penetration testing, what would present the most concern?
<--- Score

337. What type of infrastructure penetration testing is in place to gauge threats posed by both outsiders and those with inside information about the system?
<--- Score

338. Is anti-virus software installed on all servers and workstations?
<--- Score

339. What are you trying to prove to yourself, and how might it be hijacking your life and business success?
<--- Score

340. Are new benefits received and understood?
<--- Score

341. Has your organization ever been compromised (internally or externally)?
<--- Score

342. What can be attacked?
<--- Score

343. Which files have been accessed?
<--- Score

344. Do you have Network IDS on perimeter

related systems?
<--- Score

345. Is there any reason to believe the opposite of my current belief?
<--- Score

346. What are the business goals Offensive Security Certified Professional is aiming to achieve?
<--- Score

347. There is little possibility of ethical hacking in work places if information is not accurate. If a company has been hacked ethically, what is the colour of the individuals hat is it black or white?
<--- Score

348. Is a visitor log retained for at least three months to retain a log of physical activity?
<--- Score

349. What is an unauthorized commitment?
<--- Score

350. Are audit trails on all critical systems secured in a way that they cannot be tampered with?
<--- Score

351. What can an intruder see on the target systems?
<--- Score

352. Is telnet or Rlogin used for remote system administration?
<--- Score

353. What is the mission of the organization?
<--- Score

354. Ask yourself: how would we do this work if we only had one staff member to do it?
<--- Score

355. Are assumptions made in Offensive Security Certified Professional stated explicitly?
<--- Score

356. Has implementation been effective in reaching specified objectives?
<--- Score

357. Specifically, what type of remote access services does your organization use (VPN or Dial-Up RAS)?
<--- Score

358. Is access to all audit trails logged on all critical systems?
<--- Score

359. Are the criteria for selecting recommendations stated?
<--- Score

360. Who pulls the LAN cable?
<--- Score

361. Political -is anyone trying to undermine this project?
<--- Score

362. Marketing budgets are tighter, consumers are

more skeptical, and social media has changed forever the way we talk about Offensive Security Certified Professional. How do we gain traction?
<--- Score

363. Are test reports available under a non-disclosure agreement?
<--- Score

364. If there were zero limitations, what would we do differently?
<--- Score

365. Did my employees make progress today?
<--- Score

366. Who have we, as a company, historically been when we've been at our best?
<--- Score

367. Are we / should we be Revolutionary or evolutionary?
<--- Score

368. What is Tricky About This?
<--- Score

369. What was the attack?
<--- Score

370. What is normal traffic on your network?
<--- Score

371. Do you have a vision statement?
<--- Score

372. What Is The Purpose/Goal Of Penetration Testing?

<--- Score

373. Metric: did testers get access either without a password or by gaining unauthorized access to a password?

<--- Score

374. Is Offensive Security Certified Professional dependent on the successful delivery of a current project?

<--- Score

375. Are the assumptions believable and achievable?

<--- Score

376. Are information systems subject to periodic penetration tests?

<--- Score

377. What are we challenging, in the sense that Mac challenged the PC or Dove tackled the Beauty Myth?

<--- Score

378. Can we maintain our growth without detracting from the factors that have contributed to our success?

<--- Score

379. What is a feasible sequencing of reform initiatives over time?

<--- Score

380. Who will use it?

<--- Score

381. Loss of accountability - are the attackers actions traceable to an individual?
<--- Score

382. How will we ensure we get what we expected?
<--- Score

383. What is a vulnerability?
<--- Score

384. Consider the adequacy of the policy and the model for the target system. Is the model complete?
<--- Score

385. Does your organization have regularly scheduled penetration tests?
<--- Score

386. Who will manage the integration of tools?
<--- Score

387. Your reputation and success is your lifeblood, and Offensive Security Certified Professional shows you how to stay relevant, add value, and win and retain customers
<--- Score

388. Will there be any necessary staff changes (redundancies or new hires)?
<--- Score

389. Who is responsible for errors?
<--- Score

390. How is business? Why?
<--- Score

391. Does the penetration tester have experience conducting application-layer penetration testing?
<--- Score

392. Does the work address establishing secure means of communicating with the client about the engagement?
<--- Score

393. Which functions and people interact with the supplier and or customer?
<--- Score

394. When information truly is ubiquitous, when reach and connectivity are completely global, when computing resources are infinite, and when a whole new set of impossibilities are not only possible, but happening, what will that do to our business?
<--- Score

395. What are the short and long-term Offensive Security Certified Professional goals?
<--- Score

396. What are the challenges?
<--- Score

397. Are the minimum hardware components met on each network component for the software to function properly?
<--- Score

398. Has the application code been tested for vulnerabilities prior to entering production?
<--- Score

399. Were lessons learned captured and communicated?
<--- Score

400. How would our PR, marketing, and social media change if we did not use outside agencies?
<--- Score

401. What are your boundaries?
<--- Score

402. Depending on your target, can you obtain a clone of the target?
<--- Score

403. How much contingency will be available in the budget?
<--- Score

404. Do we have the right capabilities and capacities?
<--- Score

405. Are we relevant? Will we be relevant five years from now? Ten?
<--- Score

406. Is the methodology clearly stated?
<--- Score

407. What is the source of the strategies for Offensive Security Certified Professional

strengthening and reform?
<--- Score

**408. How Does Penetration Testing Relate To Other
Life Cycle Products?**
<--- Score

**409. How will you know that the Offensive Security
Certified Professional project has been successful?**
<--- Score

410. Do we say no to customers for no reason?
<--- Score

**411. Are visitors asked to sign out and turn in
badge or tag before leaving the building?**
<--- Score

**412. Think of your Offensive Security Certified
Professional project. what are the main functions?**
<--- Score

Add up total points for this section:
_ _ _ _ _ = Total points for this section

Divided by: _ _ _ _ _ _ (number of
statements answered) = _ _ _ _ _ _
Average score for this section

Transfer your score to the Offensive
Security Certified Professional Index at
the beginning of the Self-Assessment.

Offensive Security Certified Professional and Managing Projects, Criteria for Project Managers:

1.0 Initiating Process Group: Offensive Security Certified Professional

1. Were sponsors and decision makers available when needed outside regularly scheduled meetings?

2. What areas does the group agree are the biggest success on the Offensive Security Certified Professional project?

3. How well did the chosen processes fit the needs of the Offensive Security Certified Professional project?

4. Who are the Offensive Security Certified Professional project stakeholders?

5. Were resources available as planned?

6. Are the changes in your Offensive Security Certified Professional project being formally requested, analyzed, and approved by the appropriate decision makers?

7. What are the tools and techniques to be used in each phase?

8. Does the Offensive Security Certified Professional project team have enough people to execute the Offensive Security Certified Professional project plan?

9. Have you evaluated the teams performance and asked for feedback?

10. How well did the chosen processes produce the expected results?

11. If action is called for, what form should it take?

12. Do you understand the quality and control criteria that must be achieved for successful Offensive Security Certified Professional project completion?

13. Who does what?

14. What do you need to do?

15. Will the Offensive Security Certified Professional project meet the client requirements, and will it achieve the business success criteria that justified doing the Offensive Security Certified Professional project in the first place?

16. Do you know all the stakeholders impacted by the Offensive Security Certified Professional project and what needs are?

17. Who is performing the work of the Offensive Security Certified Professional project?

18. Do you know the Offensive Security Certified Professional projects goal, purpose and objectives?

19. What do they need to know about the Offensive Security Certified Professional project?

20. What are the required resources?

1.1 Project Charter: Offensive Security Certified Professional

21. What are you trying to accomplish?

22. Why have you chosen the aim you have set forth?

23. How are Offensive Security Certified Professional projects different from operations?

24. Are you building in-house ?

25. What outcome, in measureable terms, are you hoping to accomplish?

26. Market – identify products market, including whether it is outside of the objective: what is the purpose of the program or Offensive Security Certified Professional project?

27. What is the justification?

28. What are you striving to accomplish (measurable goal(s))?

29. What are the assumptions?

30. Must Have?

31. Why is it important?

32. Why do you need to manage scope?

33. Pop quiz – which are the same inputs as in the Offensive Security Certified Professional project charter?

34. Is time of the essence?

35. Why the improvements?

36. If finished, on what date did it finish?

37. Environmental stewardship and sustainability considerations: what is the process that will be used to ensure compliance with the environmental stewardship policy?

38. Success determination factors: how will the success of the Offensive Security Certified Professional project be determined from the customers perspective?

39. How will you know that a change is an improvement?

40. Does the Offensive Security Certified Professional project need to consider any special capacity or capability issues?

1.2 Stakeholder Register: Offensive Security Certified Professional

41. How will reports be created?

42. What are the major Offensive Security Certified Professional project milestones requiring communications or providing communications opportunities?

43. Who is managing stakeholder engagement?

44. Who are the stakeholders?

45. What opportunities exist to provide communications?

46. What is the power of the stakeholder?

47. How much influence do they have on the Offensive Security Certified Professional project?

48. Who wants to talk about Security?

49. What & Why?

50. Is your organization ready for change?

51. How big is the gap?

52. How should employers make voices heard?

1.3 Stakeholder Analysis Matrix: Offensive Security Certified Professional

53. How will the Offensive Security Certified Professional project benefit them?

54. Which conditions out of the control of the management are crucial for the sustainability of its effects?

55. How can you counter negative efforts?

56. Marketing - reach, distribution, awareness?

57. Identify the stakeholders levels most frequently used –or at least sought– in your Offensive Security Certified Professional projects and for which purpose?

58. Reputation, presence and reach?

59. How can you fill the need to show progress?

60. Sustainable financial backing?

61. Has there been a similar initiative in the region?

62. Usps (unique selling points)?

63. Who are potential allies and opponents?

64. Who can contribute financial or technical resources towards the work?

65. Who has not been involved up to now and should have been?

66. Which conditions out of the control of the management are crucial for the achievement of the immediate objective?

67. How to measure the achievement of the Immediate Objective?

68. Innovative aspects?

69. New technologies, services, ideas?

70. New USPs?

71. Guiding question: who shall you involve in the making of the stakeholder map?

72. Seasonality, weather effects?

2.0 Planning Process Group: Offensive Security Certified Professional

73. How are it Offensive Security Certified Professional projects different?

74. What do they need to know about the Offensive Security Certified Professional project?

75. On which process should team members spend the most time?

76. Is the pace of implementing the products of the program ensuring the completeness of the results of the Offensive Security Certified Professional project?

77. Did the program design/ implementation strategy adequately address the planning stage necessary to set up structures, hire staff etc.?

78. Is the identification of the problems, inequalities and gaps, with respective causes, clear in the Offensive Security Certified Professional project?

79. How do you integrate Offensive Security Certified Professional project Planning with the Iterative/ Evolutionary SDLC?

80. How will users learn how to use the deliverables?

81. What will you do to minimize the impact should a risk event occur?

82. Have more efficient (sensitive) and appropriate measures been adopted to respond to the political and socio-cultural problems identified?

83. Mitigate. what will you do to minimize the impact should a risk event occur?

84. Offensive Security Certified Professional project assessment; why did you do this Offensive Security Certified Professional project?

85. Is your organization showing technical capacity and leadership commitment to keep working with the Offensive Security Certified Professional project and to repeat it?

86. You are creating your WBS and find that you keep decomposing tasks into smaller and smaller units. How can you tell when you are done?

87. To what extent do the intervention objectives and strategies of the Offensive Security Certified Professional project respond to your organizations plans?

88. Product breakdown structure (pbs): what is the Offensive Security Certified Professional project result or product, and how should it look like, what are its parts?

89. What factors are contributing to progress or delay in the achievement of products and results?

90. Professionals want to know what is expected from them; what are the deliverables?

91. How will it affect you?

92. Are the necessary foundations in place to ensure the sustainability of the results of the Offensive Security Certified Professional project?

2.1 Project Management Plan: Offensive Security Certified Professional

93. Who is the sponsor?

94. What are the constraints?

95. What went wrong?

96. What should you drop in order to add something new?

97. Has the selected plan been formulated using cost effectiveness and incremental analysis techniques?

98. Who is the Offensive Security Certified Professional project Manager?

99. Are there any windfall benefits that would accrue to the Offensive Security Certified Professional project sponsor or other parties?

100. What goes into your Offensive Security Certified Professional project Charter?

101. If the Offensive Security Certified Professional project is complex or scope is specialized, do you have appropriate and/or qualified staff available to perform the tasks?

102. Is the appropriate plan selected based on your organizations objectives and evaluation criteria

expressed in Principles and Guidelines policies?

103. Is there an incremental analysis/cost effectiveness analysis of proposed mitigation features based on an approved method and using an accepted model?

104. Development trends and opportunities. What if the positive direction and vision of your organization causes expected trends to change?

105. Is mitigation authorized or recommended?

106. Are cost risk analysis methods applied to develop contingencies for the estimated total Offensive Security Certified Professional project costs?

107. Was the peer (technical) review of the cost estimates duly coordinated with the cost estimate center of expertise and addressed in the review documentation and certification?

108. Are there any client staffing expectations?

109. If the Offensive Security Certified Professional project management plan is a comprehensive document that guides you in Offensive Security Certified Professional project execution and control, then what should it NOT contain?

110. What are the known stakeholder requirements?

111. Why Change?

2.2 Scope Management Plan: Offensive Security Certified Professional

112. Materials available for performing the work?

113. Have Offensive Security Certified Professional project management standards and procedures been identified / established and documented?

114. Are assumptions being identified, recorded, analyzed, qualified and closed?

115. Are there procedures in place to effectively manage interdependencies with other Offensive Security Certified Professional projects, systems, Vendors and your organizations work effort?

116. Is there an issues management plan in place?

117. Are enough systems & user personnel assigned to the Offensive Security Certified Professional project?

118. Time estimation – how much time will be needed?

119. Why is a scope management plan important?

120. Does the Offensive Security Certified Professional project have a Statement of Work?

121. Are vendor contract reports, reviews and visits

conducted periodically?

122. Knowing the health of the Offensive Security Certified Professional project – What is the status?

123. Are multiple estimation methods being employed?

124. What is the estimated cost of creating and implementing?

125. Have all team members been part of identifying risks?

126. Describe the process for rejecting the Offensive Security Certified Professional project deliverables. What happens to rejected deliverables?

127. Which statement about customer expectations is not true?

128. Are the quality tools and methods identified in the Quality Plan appropriate to the Offensive Security Certified Professional project?

129. Are Offensive Security Certified Professional project leaders committed to this Offensive Security Certified Professional project full time?

130. Are funding resource estimates sufficiently detailed and documented for use in planning and tracking the Offensive Security Certified Professional project?

2.3 Requirements Management Plan: Offensive Security Certified Professional

131. Has the requirements team been instructed in the Change Control process?

132. The wbs is developed as part of a joint planning session. and how do you know that youhave done this right?

133. Will the contractors involved take full responsibility?

134. Did you provide clear and concise specifications?

135. Describe the process for rejecting the Offensive Security Certified Professional project requirements. Who has the authority to reject Offensive Security Certified Professional project requirements?

136. How will the requirements become prioritized?

137. Should you include sub-activities?

138. In case of software development; Should you have a test for each code module?

139. If it exists, where is it housed?

140. Does the Offensive Security Certified Professional project have a Change Control process?

141. How will you develop the schedule of requirements activities?

142. How will bidders price evaluations be done, by deliverables, phases, or in a big bang?

143. Did you avoid subjective, flowery or non-specific statements?

144. How knowledgeable is the primary Stakeholder(s) in the proposed application area?

145. Will the Offensive Security Certified Professional project requirements become approved in writing?

146. Is any organizational data being used or stored?

147. Did you use declarative statements?

148. How will the information be distributed?

149. Is stakeholder risk tolerance an important factor for the requirements process in this Offensive Security Certified Professional project?

2.4 Requirements Documentation: Offensive Security Certified Professional

150. Does the system provide the functions which best support the customers needs?

151. Consistency. are there any requirements conflicts?

152. Is new technology needed?

153. How do you know when a Requirement is accurate enough?

154. What facilities must be supported by the system?

155. Can the requirement be changed without a large impact on other requirements?

156. Are all functions required by the customer included?

157. What variations exist for a process?

158. Have the benefits identified with the system being identified clearly?

159. What can tools do for us?

160. How will they be documented / shared?

161. What are current process problems?

162. How does the proposed Offensive Security Certified Professional project contribute to the overall objectives of your organization?

163. Are there legal issues?

164. Is the requirement properly understood?

165. The problem with gathering requirements is right there in the word gathering. What images does it conjure?

166. Who is interacting with the system?

167. Can the requirements be checked?

168. Who provides requirements?

169. How much does requirements engineering cost?

2.5 Requirements Traceability Matrix: Offensive Security Certified Professional

170. Why use a WBS?

171. How do you manage scope?

172. How small is small enough?

173. What are the chronologies, contingencies, consequences, criteria?

174. Will you use a Requirements Traceability Matrix?

175. What is the WBS?

176. Do you have a clear understanding of all subcontracts in place?

177. How will it affect the stakeholders personally in their career?

178. What percentage of Offensive Security Certified Professional projects are producing traceability matrices between requirements and other work products?

179. Is there a requirements traceability process in place?

180. Why do you manage scope?

181. Describe the process for approving requirements so they can be added to the traceability matrix and Offensive Security Certified Professional project work can be performed. Will the Offensive Security Certified Professional project requirements become approved in writing?

2.6 Project Scope Statement: Offensive Security Certified Professional

182. Is there a Change Management Board?

183. Have you been able to thoroughly document the Offensive Security Certified Professional projects assumptions and constraints?

184. Is there an information system for the Offensive Security Certified Professional project?

185. Will the Offensive Security Certified Professional project risks be managed according to the Offensive Security Certified Professional projects risk management process?

186. If the scope changes, what will the impact be to your Offensive Security Certified Professional project in terms of duration, cost, quality, or any other important areas of the Offensive Security Certified Professional project?

187. Where and how does the team fit within your organization structure?

188. If there is an independent oversight contractor, have they signed off on the Offensive Security Certified Professional project Plan?

189. Is an issue management process documented and filed?

190. Identify how your team and you will create the Offensive Security Certified Professional project scope statement and the work breakdown structure (WBS). Document how you will create the Offensive Security Certified Professional project scope statement and WBS, and make sure you answer the following questions: In defining Offensive Security Certified Professional project scope and the WBS, will you and your Offensive Security Certified Professional project team be using methods defined by your organization, methods defined by the Offensive Security Certified Professional project management office (PMO), or other methods?

191. Is the change control process documented and on file?

192. Risks?

193. Has everyone approved the Offensive Security Certified Professional projects scope statement?

194. Will an issue form be in use?

195. Is the Offensive Security Certified Professional project sponsor function identified and defined?

196. Is the Offensive Security Certified Professional project manager qualified and experienced in Offensive Security Certified Professional project management?

197. How often will scope changes be reviewed?

198. Is the Offensive Security Certified Professional

project organization documented and on file?

2.7 Assumption and Constraint Log: Offensive Security Certified Professional

199. Have adequate resources been provided by management to ensure Offensive Security Certified Professional project success?

200. What is positive about the current process?

201. Are there processes in place to ensure that all the terms and code concepts have been documented consistently?

202. Is staff trained on the software technologies that are being used on the Offensive Security Certified Professional project?

203. Security analysis has access to information that is sanitized?

204. Are there processes defining how software will be developed including development methods, overall timeline for development, software product standards, and traceability?

205. If it is out of compliance, should the process be amended or should the Plan be amended?

206. How can you prevent/fix violations?

207. What if failure during recovery?

208. No superfluous information or marketing narrative?

209. Do you know what your customers expectations are regarding this process?

210. Is the definition of the Offensive Security Certified Professional project scope clear; what needs to be accomplished?

211. Does the document/deliverable meet all requirements (for example, statement of work) specific to this deliverable?

212. What worked well?

213. Has a Offensive Security Certified Professional project Communications Plan been developed?

214. Do documented requirements exist for all critical components and areas, including technical, business, interfaces, performance, security and conversion requirements?

215. Is the steering committee active in Offensive Security Certified Professional project oversight?

216. Are there nonconformance issues?

217. Does a documented Offensive Security Certified Professional project organizational policy & plan (i.e. governance model) exist?

218. Are there procedures in place to effectively manage interdependencies with other Offensive Security Certified Professional projects / systems?

2.8 Work Breakdown Structure: Offensive Security Certified Professional

219. Why would you develop a Work Breakdown Structure?

220. When does it have to be done?

221. When would you develop a Work Breakdown Structure?

222. Can you make it?

223. Why is it useful?

224. Where does it take place?

225. Who has to do it?

226. What has to be done?

227. Is it still viable?

228. What is the probability of completing the Offensive Security Certified Professional project in less that xx days?

229. How will you and your Offensive Security Certified Professional project team define the Offensive Security Certified Professional projects scope and work breakdown structure?

230. How many levels?

231. How much detail?

232. When do you stop?

233. Do you need another level?

234. Is it a change in scope?

235. How far down?

236. Is the work breakdown structure (wbs) defined and is the scope of the Offensive Security Certified Professional project clear with assigned deliverable owners?

237. What is the probability that the Offensive Security Certified Professional project duration will exceed xx weeks?

238. How big is a work-package?

2.9 WBS Dictionary: Offensive Security Certified Professional

239. Changes in the nature of the overhead requirements?

240. Are data elements (BCWS, BCWP, and ACWP) progressively summarized from the detail level to the contract level through the CWBS?

241. Is cost and schedule performance measurement done in a consistent, systematic manner?

242. Is the work done on a work package level as described in the WBS dictionary?

243. Are the bases and rates for allocating costs from each indirect pool to commercial work consistent with the already stated used to allocate corresponding costs to Government contracts?

244. Does the contractors system provide for accurate cost accumulation and assignment to control accounts in a manner consistent with the budgets using recognized acceptable costing techniques?

245. Are the rates for allocating costs from each indirect cost pool to contracts updated as necessary to ensure a realistic monthly allocation of indirect costs without significant year-end adjustments?

246. Is cost performance measurement at the point in time most suitable for the category of material

involved, and no earlier than the time of actual receipt of material?

247. Are overhead cost budgets (or Offensive Security Certified Professional projections) established on a facility-wide basis at least annually for the life of the contract?

248. Are material costs reported within the same period as that in which BCWP is earned for that material?

249. The anticipated business volume?

250. What is the end result of a work package?

251. What went right?

252. Knowledgeable Offensive Security Certified Professional projections of future performance?

253. Are the bases and rates for allocating costs from each indirect pool consistently applied?

254. All cwbs elements specified for external reporting?

255. Are records maintained to show how management reserves are used?

256. Identify and isolate causes of favorable and unfavorable cost and schedule variances?

2.10 Schedule Management Plan: Offensive Security Certified Professional

257. Is there a procedure for management, control and release of schedule margin?

258. Are tasks tracked by hours?

259. Does the ims reflect accurate current status and credible start/finish forecasts for all to-go tasks and milestones?

260. Have Offensive Security Certified Professional project success criteria been defined?

261. Are there checklists created to determine if all quality processes are followed?

262. Is the communication plan being followed?

263. Are Offensive Security Certified Professional project team members involved in detailed estimating and scheduling?

264. Define units of measurement for each resource. For example, are you referencing gallons or liters?

265. Have the key elements of a coherent Offensive Security Certified Professional project management strategy been established?

266. Were Offensive Security Certified Professional

project team members involved in the development of activity & task decomposition?

267. Were the budget estimates reasonable?

268. Is the steering committee active in Offensive Security Certified Professional project oversight?

269. Are procurement deliverables arriving on time and to specification?

270. Are there any activities or deliverables being added or gold-plated that could be dropped or scaled back without falling short of the original requirement?

271. Has the Offensive Security Certified Professional project scope been baselined?

272. What is the difference between % Complete and % work?

273. Quality assurance overheads?

274. Has the ims been resource-loaded and are assigned resources reasonable and available?

275. Are the predecessor and successor relationships accurate?

276. Is the quality assurance team identified?

2.11 Activity List: Offensive Security Certified Professional

277. What is your organizations history in doing similar activities?

278. What are you counting on?

279. What is the total time required to complete the Offensive Security Certified Professional project if no delays occur?

280. What will be performed?

281. When do the individual activities need to start and finish?

282. Where will it be performed?

283. Who will perform the work?

284. Is infrastructure setup part of your Offensive Security Certified Professional project?

285. Is there anything planned that does not need to be here?

286. How do you determine the late start (LS) for each activity?

287. How difficult will it be to do specific activities on this Offensive Security Certified Professional project?

288. Are the required resources available or need to be acquired?

289. How should ongoing costs be monitored to try to keep the Offensive Security Certified Professional project within budget?

290. What is the LF and LS for each activity?

291. For other activities, how much delay can be tolerated?

292. What are the critical bottleneck activities?

2.12 Activity Attributes: Offensive Security Certified Professional

293. How difficult will it be to do specific activities on this Offensive Security Certified Professional project?

294. Are the required resources available?

295. Does your organization of the data change its meaning?

296. How many days do you need to complete the work scope with a limit of X number of resources?

297. Can more resources be added?

298. What conclusions/generalizations can you draw from this?

299. Is there a trend during the year?

300. Where else does it apply?

301. Activity: fair or not fair?

302. Have constraints been applied to the start and finish milestones for the phases?

303. Time for overtime?

304. What is the general pattern here?

305. Were there other ways you could have organized

the data to achieve similar results?

306. Resources to accomplish the work?

307. What activity do you think you should spend the most time on?

308. Do you feel very comfortable with your prediction?

2.13 Milestone List: Offensive Security Certified Professional

309. Global influences?

310. Effects on core activities, distraction?

311. Legislative effects?

312. What background experience, skills, and strengths does the team bring to your organization?

313. Can you derive how soon can the whole Offensive Security Certified Professional project finish?

314. Describe your organizations strengths and core competencies. What factors will make your organization succeed?

315. Sustaining internal capabilities?

316. Identify critical paths (one or more) and which activities are on the critical path?

317. How difficult will it be to do specific activities on this Offensive Security Certified Professional project?

318. Continuity, supply chain robustness?

319. How will the milestone be verified?

320. Information and research?

321. Level of the Innovation?

322. Timescales, deadlines and pressures?

323. How soon can the activity finish?

324. Obstacles faced?

325. When will the Offensive Security Certified Professional project be complete?

326. Environmental effects?

2.14 Network Diagram: Offensive Security Certified Professional

327. Review the logical flow of the network diagram. Take a look at which activities you have first and then sequence the activities. Do they make sense?

328. How confident can you be in your milestone dates and the delivery date?

329. Will crashing x weeks return more in benefits than it costs?

330. Exercise: what is the probability that the Offensive Security Certified Professional project duration will exceed xx weeks?

331. What activities must occur simultaneously with this activity?

332. Planning: who, how long, what to do?

333. Can you calculate the confidence level?

334. How difficult will it be to do specific activities on this Offensive Security Certified Professional project?

335. If x is long, what would be the completion time if you break x into two parallel parts of y weeks and z weeks?

336. Which type of network diagram allows you to depict four types of dependencies?

337. What can be done concurrently?

338. If the Offensive Security Certified Professional project network diagram cannot change and you have extra personnel resources, what is the BEST thing to do?

339. What to do and When?

340. What is the completion time?

341. What are the Major Administrative Issues?

342. What must be completed before an activity can be started?

343. What job or jobs follow it?

344. What job or jobs could run concurrently?

2.15 Activity Resource Requirements: Offensive Security Certified Professional

345. What are constraints that you might find during the Human Resource Planning process?

346. When does monitoring begin?

347. Do you use tools like decomposition and rolling-wave planning to produce the activity list and other outputs?

348. Organizational Applicability?

349. Are there unresolved issues that need to be addressed?

350. Other support in specific areas?

351. How do you manage time?

352. How do you handle petty cash?

353. How many signatures do you require on a check and does this match what is in your policy and procedures?

354. Why do you do that?

355. Anything else?

356. Which logical relationship does the PDM use

most often?

357. What is the Work Plan Standard?

2.16 Resource Breakdown Structure: Offensive Security Certified Professional

358. Who will use the system?

359. Is predictive resource analysis being done?

360. Why is this important?

361. What is Offensive Security Certified Professional project communication management?

362. Why do you do it?

363. Changes based on input from stakeholders?

364. How can this help you with team building?

365. How difficult will it be to do specific activities on this Offensive Security Certified Professional project?

366. Who will be used as a Offensive Security Certified Professional project team member?

367. Goals for the Offensive Security Certified Professional project. What is each stakeholders desired outcome for the Offensive Security Certified Professional project?

368. Any changes from stakeholders?

369. Which resource planning tool provides

information on resource responsibility and accountability?

370. Who is allowed to perform which functions?

371. What are the requirements for resource data?

372. Who is allowed to see what data about which resources?

2.17 Activity Duration Estimates: Offensive Security Certified Professional

373. Are activity duration estimates documented?

374. Total slack can be calculated by which equations?

375. How do you enter durations, link tasks, and view critical path information?

376. Can they use the already stated?

377. Is a contract change control system defined to manage changes to contract terms and conditions?

378. Are operational definitions created to identify quality measurement criteria for specific activities?

379. Are inspections completed to determine if the results comply with the requirements?

380. What are the three main outputs of quality control?

381. Are procurement documents used to solicit accurate and complete proposals from prospective sellers?

382. Which is the BEST Offensive Security Certified Professional project management tool to use to determine the longest time the Offensive Security Certified Professional project will take?

383. Will it help in finding or retaining employees?

384. Are time, scope, cost, and quality monitored throughout the Offensive Security Certified Professional project?

385. If Offensive Security Certified Professional project time and cost are not as important as the number of resources used each month, which is the BEST thing to do?

386. Is a Offensive Security Certified Professional project charter created once a Offensive Security Certified Professional project is formally recognized?

387. What steps did your organization take to earn this prestigious quality award?

388. Research recruiting and retention strategies at three different companies. What distinguishes one organization from another in this area?

389. Are training needs identified when resources do not have the required skills to complete Offensive Security Certified Professional project activities?

390. Briefly summarize the work done by Maslow, Herzberg, McClellan, McGregor, Ouchi, Thamhain and Wilemon, and Covey. How do theories relate to Offensive Security Certified Professional project management?

391. Explanation notice how many choices are half right?

392. Will the new application negatively affect the current IT infrastructure?

2.18 Duration Estimating Worksheet: Offensive Security Certified Professional

393. How should ongoing costs be monitored to try to keep the Offensive Security Certified Professional project within budget?

394. When does your organization expect to be able to complete it?

395. Small or large Offensive Security Certified Professional project?

396. What info is needed?

397. Why estimate time and cost?

398. What is cost and Offensive Security Certified Professional project cost management?

399. What is the total time required to complete the Offensive Security Certified Professional project if no delays occur?

400. Will the Offensive Security Certified Professional project collaborate with the local community and leverage resources?

401. Value pocket identification & quantification what are value pockets?

402. What is your role?

403. Is this operation cost effective?

404. Is the Offensive Security Certified Professional project responsive to community need?

405. Do any colleagues have experience with your organization and/or RFPs?

406. What is an Average Offensive Security Certified Professional project?

407. Is a construction detail attached (to aid in explanation)?

408. What utility impacts are there?

409. How can the Offensive Security Certified Professional project be displayed graphically to better visualize the activities?

2.19 Project Schedule: Offensive Security Certified Professional

410. If you can not fix it, how do you do it differently?

411. Offensive Security Certified Professional project work estimates Who is managing the work estimate quality of work tasks in the Offensive Security Certified Professional project schedule?

412. Did the Offensive Security Certified Professional project come in under budget?

413. How effectively were issues able to be resolved without impacting the Offensive Security Certified Professional project Schedule or Budget?

414. Eliminate unnecessary activities. Are there activities that came from a template or previous Offensive Security Certified Professional project that are not applicable on this phase of this Offensive Security Certified Professional project?

415. Why do you need to manage Offensive Security Certified Professional project Risk?

416. Is the structure for tracking the Offensive Security Certified Professional project schedule well defined and assigned to a specific individual?

417. Why is this particularly bad?

418. Why do you think schedule issues often cause

the most conflicts on Offensive Security Certified Professional projects?

419. Did the final product meet or exceed user expectations?

420. To what degree is do you feel the entire team was committed to the Offensive Security Certified Professional project schedule?

421. What is the purpose of a Offensive Security Certified Professional project schedule?

422. How can slack be negative?

423. Your Offensive Security Certified Professional project management plan results in a Offensive Security Certified Professional project schedule that is too long. If the Offensive Security Certified Professional project network diagram cannot change and you have extra personnel resources, what is the BEST thing to do?

424. Is there a Schedule Management Plan that establishes the criteria and activities for developing, monitoring and controlling the Offensive Security Certified Professional project schedule?

425. What is Offensive Security Certified Professional project management?

426. What is risk?

427. Change management required?

428. Is infrastructure setup part of your Offensive

Security Certified Professional project?

429. Your best shot for providing estimations how complex/how much work does the activity require?

2.20 Cost Management Plan: Offensive Security Certified Professional

430. Are all resource assumptions documented?

431. Has a provision been made to reassess Offensive Security Certified Professional project risks at various Offensive Security Certified Professional project stages?

432. Are Offensive Security Certified Professional project team members involved in detailed estimating and scheduling?

433. Is there a formal set of procedures supporting Issues Management?

434. Sensitivity analysis?

435. Are updated Offensive Security Certified Professional project time & resource estimates reasonable based on the current Offensive Security Certified Professional project stage?

436. Are Offensive Security Certified Professional project leaders committed to this Offensive Security Certified Professional project full time?

437. Are adequate resources provided for the quality assurance function?

438. Are schedule deliverables actually delivered?

439. Are issues raised, assessed, actioned, and resolved in a timely and efficient manner?

440. Offensive Security Certified Professional project definition & scope?

441. The definition of the Offensive Security Certified Professional project scope what needs to be accomplished?

442. Is there a Steering Committee in place?

443. Are decisions captured in a decisions log?

444. Is a stakeholder management plan in place that covers topics?

445. Was your organizations estimating methodology being used and followed?

446. Are the Offensive Security Certified Professional project plans updated on a frequent basis?

447. Forecasts – how will the time and resources needed to complete the Offensive Security Certified Professional project be forecast?

448. Does a documented Offensive Security Certified Professional project organizational policy & plan (i.e. governance model) exist?

449. Exclusions – is there scope to be performed or provided by others?

2.21 Activity Cost Estimates: Offensive Security Certified Professional

450. How Award?

451. What were things that you did very well and want to do the same again on the next Offensive Security Certified Professional project?

452. What cost data should be used to estimate costs during the 2-year follow-up period?

453. Review – what are some common errors in activities to avoid?

454. What are you looking for?

455. What areas does the group agree are the biggest success on the Offensive Security Certified Professional project?

456. When do you enter into PPM?

457. Are cost subtotals needed?

458. What is the estimators estimating history?

459. One way to define activities is to consider how organization employees describe jobs to families and friends. You basically want to know, What do you do?

460. Did the consultant work with local staff to develop local capacity?

461. What areas were overlooked on this Offensive Security Certified Professional project?

462. Does the estimator estimate by task or by person?

463. What makes a good activity description?

464. What is the last item a Offensive Security Certified Professional project manager must do to finalize Offensive Security Certified Professional project close-out?

465. What procedures are put in place regarding bidding and cost comparisons, if any?

466. Who determines when the contractor is paid?

467. Certification of actual expenditures?

468. Padding is bad and contingencies are good. what is the difference?

2.22 Cost Estimating Worksheet: Offensive Security Certified Professional

469. What happens to any remaining funds not used?

470. Can a trend be established from historical performance data on the selected measure and are the criteria for using trend analysis or forecasting methods met?

471. What can be included?

472. What costs are to be estimated?

473. Will the Offensive Security Certified Professional project collaborate with the local community and leverage resources?

474. Is it feasible to establish a control group arrangement?

475. Does the Offensive Security Certified Professional project provide innovative ways for stakeholders to overcome obstacles or deliver better outcomes?

476. Who is best positioned to know and assist in identifying corresponding factors?

477. How will the results be shared and to whom?

478. Is the Offensive Security Certified Professional project responsive to community need?

479. What additional Offensive Security Certified Professional project(s) could be initiated as a result of this Offensive Security Certified Professional project?

480. What is the estimated labor cost today based upon this information?

481. What is the purpose of estimating?

482. Identify the timeframe necessary to monitor progress and collect data to determine how the selected measure has changed?

483. Ask: are others positioned to know, are others credible, and will others cooperate?

484. What will others want?

2.23 Cost Baseline: Offensive Security Certified Professional

485. Pcs for your new business. what would the life cycle costs be?

486. How difficult will it be to do specific tasks on the Offensive Security Certified Professional project?

487. Have all approved changes to the cost baseline been identified and impact on the Offensive Security Certified Professional project documented?

488. Verify business objectives. Are others appropriate, and well-articulated?

489. Has operations management formally accepted responsibility for operating and maintaining the product(s) or service(s) delivered by the Offensive Security Certified Professional project?

490. What is it ?

491. Is the cr within Offensive Security Certified Professional project scope?

492. Have all approved changes to the Offensive Security Certified Professional project requirement been identified and impact on the performance, cost, and schedule baselines documented?

493. Why do you manage cost?

494. Will the Offensive Security Certified Professional project fail if the change request is not executed?

495. What strengths do you have?

496. Vac -variance at completion, how much over/ under budget do you expect to be?

497. Have the lessons learned been filed with the Offensive Security Certified Professional project Management Office?

498. Who will use corresponding metrics ?

499. Have you identified skills that are missing from your team?

500. What can go wrong?

501. Is request in line with priorities?

502. Has the Offensive Security Certified Professional projected annual cost to operate and maintain the product(s) or service(s) been approved and funded?

503. How concrete were original objectives?

2.24 Quality Management Plan: Offensive Security Certified Professional

504. You know what your customers expectations are regarding this process?

505. How does your organization make it easy for customers to seek assistance or complain?

506. How is staff informed of proper reporting methods?

507. What methods are used?

508. Have you eliminated all duplicative tasks or manual efforts, where appropriate?

509. How do senior leaders review organizational performance?

510. Contradictory information between different documents?

511. How do you ensure that your sampling methods and procedures meet your data needs?

512. How do senior leaders create your organizational focus on customers and other stakeholders?

513. Does a documented Offensive Security Certified Professional project organizational policy & plan (i.e. governance model) exist?

514. How does your organization establish and maintain customer relationships?

515. When reporting to different audiences, do you vary the form or type of report?

516. Is the steering committee active in Offensive Security Certified Professional project oversight?

517. Were there any deficiencies / issues identified in the prior years self-assessment?

518. Are decisions/actions based on data collected?

519. How does your organization decide what to measure?

520. Does the program conduct field testing?

521. How are new requirements or changes to requirements identified?

522. How do you decide what information to record?

2.25 Quality Metrics: Offensive Security Certified Professional

523. Which data do others need in one place to target areas of improvement?

524. What are your organizations expectations for its quality Offensive Security Certified Professional project?

525. Who is willing to lead?

526. Has trace of defects been initiated?

527. How does one achieve stability?

528. Filter visualizations of interest?

529. Did evaluation start on time?

530. Does risk analysis documentation meet standards?

531. What forces exist that would cause them to change?

532. Has risk analysis been adequately reviewed?

533. Do you know how much profit a 10% decrease in waste would generate?

534. Is quality culture a competitive advantage?

535. Subjective quality component: customer satisfaction, how do you measure it?

536. What makes a visualization memorable?

537. There are many reasons to shore up quality-related metrics, and what metrics are important?

538. What happens if you get an abnormal result?

539. Is there a set of procedures to capture, analyze and act on quality metrics?

540. What documentation is required?

541. The metrics–what is being considered?

542. Who notifies stakeholders of normal and abnormal results?

2.26 Process Improvement Plan: Offensive Security Certified Professional

543. Are there forms and procedures to collect and record the data?

544. Purpose of goal: the motive is determined by asking, why do you want to achieve this goal?

545. Modeling current processes is great, and will you ever see a return on that investment?

546. What personnel are the change agents for your initiative?

547. The motive is determined by asking, Why do you want to achieve this goal?

548. Does explicit definition of the measures exist?

549. Have the supporting tools been developed or acquired?

550. Where are you now?

551. What is the return on investment?

552. Are you making progress on the goals?

553. Are you meeting the quality standards?

554. What personnel are the coaches for your

initiative?

555. What makes people good SPI coaches?

556. If a process improvement framework is being used, which elements will help the problems and goals listed?

557. Does your process ensure quality?

558. Why quality management?

559. To elicit goal statements, do you ask a question such as, What do you want to achieve?

560. What lessons have you learned so far?

561. Where do you want to be?

562. What personnel are the champions for the initiative?

2.27 Responsibility Assignment Matrix: Offensive Security Certified Professional

563. Contract line items and end items?

564. The already stated responsible for the establishment of budgets and assignment of resources for overhead performance?

565. Who is going to do that work?

566. Who is responsible for work and budgets for each wbs?

567. Actual cost of work performed?

568. Does the accounting system provide a basis for auditing records of direct costs chargeable to the contract?

569. Are the actual costs used for variance analysis reconcilable with data from the accounting system?

570. Are significant decision points, constraints, and interfaces identified as key milestones?

571. What tool can show you individual and group allocations?

572. Are meaningful indicators identified for use in measuring the status of cost and schedule performance?

573. Does the contractor use objective results, design reviews, and tests to trace schedule?

574. Are others working on the right things?

575. Does the contractors system provide unit or lot costs when applicable?

576. How cost benefit analysis?

577. Are records maintained to show how undistributed budgets are controlled?

578. The staff characteristics – is the group or the person capable to work together as a team?

579. Are estimates of costs at completion generated in a rational, consistent manner?

580. Offensive Security Certified Professional projected economic escalation?

581. Where does all this information come from?

2.28 Roles and Responsibilities: Offensive Security Certified Professional

582. To decide whether to use a quality measurement, ask how will you know when it is achieved?

583. Accountabilities: what are the roles and responsibilities of individual team members?

584. What areas of supervision are challenging for you?

585. Key conclusions and recommendations: Are conclusions and recommendations relevant and acceptable?

586. Are governance roles and responsibilities documented?

587. Do you take the time to clearly define roles and responsibilities on Offensive Security Certified Professional project tasks?

588. Attainable / achievable: the goal is attainable; can you actually accomplish the goal?

589. What should you do now to ensure that you are exceeding expectations and excelling in your current position?

590. Are Offensive Security Certified Professional project team roles and responsibilities identified and

documented?

591. Influence: what areas of organizational decision making are you able to influence when you do not have authority to make the final decision?

592. Once the responsibilities are defined for the Offensive Security Certified Professional project, have the deliverables, roles and responsibilities been clearly communicated to every participant?

593. What are your major roles and responsibilities in the area of performance measurement and assessment?

594. Was the expectation clearly communicated?

595. What areas would you highlight for changes or improvements?

596. Required skills, knowledge, experience?

597. Do the values and practices inherent in the culture of your organization foster or hinder the process?

598. Is the data complete?

599. How is your work-life balance?

600. What is working well?

2.29 Human Resource Management Plan: Offensive Security Certified Professional

601. Does the resource management plan include a personnel development plan?

602. Is there an on-going process in place to monitor Offensive Security Certified Professional project risks?

603. Do you have the reasons why the changes to your organizational systems and capabilities are required?

604. Are software metrics formally captured, analyzed and used as a basis for other Offensive Security Certified Professional project estimates?

605. Where is your organization headed?

606. Are the key elements of a Offensive Security Certified Professional project Charter present?

607. Have external dependencies been captured in the schedule?

608. Does the business case include how the Offensive Security Certified Professional project aligns with your organizations strategic goals & objectives?

609. Are all key components of a Quality Assurance Plan present?

610. Are Offensive Security Certified Professional project team roles and responsibilities identified and documented?

611. Is there any form of automated support for Issues Management?

612. Has the budget been baselined?

613. Are the Offensive Security Certified Professional project team members located locally to the users/stakeholders?

614. What areas were overlooked on this Offensive Security Certified Professional project?

615. Are quality metrics defined?

616. Are quality inspections and review activities listed in the Offensive Security Certified Professional project schedule(s)?

617. Is the Offensive Security Certified Professional project sponsor clearly communicating the business case or rationale for why this Offensive Security Certified Professional project is needed?

618. Account for the purpose of this Offensive Security Certified Professional project by describing, at a high-level, what will be done. What is this Offensive Security Certified Professional project aiming to achieve?

619. Are cause and effect determined for risks when others occur?

2.30 Communications Management Plan: Offensive Security Certified Professional

620. What communications method?

621. Are there common objectives between the team and the stakeholder?

622. Are stakeholders internal or external?

623. Why do you manage communications?

624. Where do team members get information?

625. Do you prepare stakeholder engagement plans?

626. What to know?

627. Is there an important stakeholder who is actively opposed and will not receive messages?

628. Are there potential barriers between the team and the stakeholder?

629. What is Offensive Security Certified Professional project communications management?

630. Do you have members of your team responsible for certain stakeholders?

631. Are there too many who have an interest in some aspect of your work?

632. Which stakeholders are thought leaders, influences, or early adopters?

633. What does the stakeholder need from the team?

634. What help do you and your team need from the stakeholder?

635. How is this initiative related to other portfolios, programs, or Offensive Security Certified Professional projects?

636. What to learn?

637. Do you then often overlook a key stakeholder or stakeholder group?

638. Who will use or be affected by the result of a Offensive Security Certified Professional project?

639. Are others part of the communications management plan?

2.31 Risk Management Plan: Offensive Security Certified Professional

640. Are people attending meetings and doing work?

641. Are some people working on multiple Offensive Security Certified Professional projects?

642. Does the software engineering team have the right mix of skills?

643. Have you worked with the customer in the past?

644. Are the software tools integrated with each other?

645. Are testing tools available and suitable?

646. Financial risk -can your organization afford to undertake the Offensive Security Certified Professional project?

647. Degree of confidence in estimated size estimate?

648. Do you train all developers in the process?

649. What is the impact to the Offensive Security Certified Professional project if the item is not resolved in a timely fashion?

650. Are enough people available?

651. Is there anything you would now do differently on your Offensive Security Certified Professional project based on this experience?

652. Is the customer technically sophisticated in the product area?

653. Risk documentation: what reporting formats and processes will be used for risk management activities?

654. Are certain activities taking a long time to complete?

655. How can the process be made more effective or less cumbersome (process improvements)?

656. Prioritized components/features?

657. What is the probability the risk avoidance strategy will be successful?

658. Who/what can assist?

2.32 Risk Register: Offensive Security Certified Professional

659. What could prevent you delivering on the strategic program objectives and what is being done to mitigate corresponding issues?

660. Methodology: how will risk management be performed on this Offensive Security Certified Professional project?

661. Do you require further engagement?

662. Are your objectives at risk?

663. What are you going to do to limit the Offensive Security Certified Professional projects risk exposure due to the identified risks?

664. What evidence do you have to justify the likelihood score of the risk (audit, incident report, claim, complaints, inspection, internal review)?

665. Budget and schedule: what are the estimated costs and schedules for performing risk-related activities?

666. What can be done about it?

667. What is the reason for current performance gaps and do the risks and opportunities identified previously account for this?

668. Who is accountable?

669. How could corresponding Risk affect the Offensive Security Certified Professional project in terms of cost and schedule?

670. Assume the risk event or situation happens, what would the impact be?

671. Is further information required before making a decision?

672. What has changed since the last period?

673. How are risks graded?

674. Why would you develop a risk register?

675. Are there any gaps in the evidence?

676. How well are risks controlled?

677. How often will the Risk Management Plan and Risk Register be formally reviewed, and by whom?

678. Risk categories: what are the main categories of risks that should be addressed on this Offensive Security Certified Professional project?

2.33 Probability and Impact Assessment: Offensive Security Certified Professional

679. What is the probability of the risk occurring?

680. Do you use any methods to analyze risks?

681. Who should be notified of the occurrence of each of the risk indicators?

682. Do the requirements require the creation of new algorithms?

683. Can you avoid altogether some things that might go wrong?

684. What should be the external organizations responsibility vis-à-vis total stake in the Offensive Security Certified Professional project?

685. What are the preparations required for facing difficulties?

686. Risk categorization -which of your categories has more risk than others?

687. What kind of preparation would be required to do this?

688. Which role do you have in the Offensive Security Certified Professional project?

689. Are there any Offensive Security Certified Professional projects similar to this one in existence?

690. Are there new risks that mitigation strategies might introduce?

691. My Offensive Security Certified Professional project leader has suddenly left your organization, what do you do?

692. Are team members trained in the use of the tools?

693. What are the current or emerging trends of culture?

694. What new technologies are being explored in the same area?

695. Which of your Offensive Security Certified Professional projects should be selected when compared with other Offensive Security Certified Professional projects?

696. Mitigation -how can you avoid the risk?

697. Costs associated with late delivery or a defective product?

2.34 Probability and Impact Matrix: Offensive Security Certified Professional

698. What are the chances the event will occur?

699. Are you on schedule?

700. Does the customer have a solid idea of what is required?

701. What should be the level of coordination?

702. Are compilers and code generators available and suitable for the product to be built?

703. What should be the level of difficulty in handling the technology?

704. Were there any Offensive Security Certified Professional projects similar to this one in existence?

705. Do requirements demand the use of new analysis, design, or testing methods?

706. What is the best method for analysing the risks for different types of Offensive Security Certified Professional projects?

707. Maximize short-term return on investment?

708. Are formal technical reviews part of this process?

709. Is the customer willing to participate in reviews?

710. Are flexibility and reuse paramount?

711. Do you have a mechanism for managing change?

712. Number of users of the product?

713. Who are the owners?

2.35 Risk Data Sheet: Offensive Security Certified Professional

714. Is the data sufficiently specified in terms of the type of failure being analyzed, and its frequency or probability?

715. Will revised controls lead to tolerable risk levels?

716. What was measured?

717. What are you trying to achieve (Objectives)?

718. What can happen?

719. What will be the consequences if it happens?

720. What are the main opportunities available to you that you should grab while you can?

721. Risk of what?

722. Type of risk identified?

723. Do effective diagnostic tests exist?

724. What are the main threats to your existence?

725. What were the Causes that contributed?

726. How can hazards be reduced?

727. How reliable is the data source?

728. What do people affected think about the need for, and practicality of preventive measures?

729. What is the environment within which you operate (social trends, economic, community values, broad based participation, national directions etc.)?

730. How can it happen?

731. Are new hazards created?

732. What is the chance that it will happen?

733. What if client refuses?

2.36 Procurement Management Plan: Offensive Security Certified Professional

734. Are actuals compared against estimates to analyze and correct variances?

735. Is pert / critical path or equivalent methodology being used?

736. Is there a formal process for updating the Offensive Security Certified Professional project baseline?

737. Is there a procurement management plan in place?

738. Are estimating assumptions and constraints captured?

739. Measurable - are the targets measurable?

740. Does the Offensive Security Certified Professional project have a Statement of Work?

741. Are the appropriate IT resources adequate to meet planned commitments?

742. Were Offensive Security Certified Professional project team members involved in detailed estimating and scheduling?

743. Are the Offensive Security Certified Professional

project plans updated on a frequent basis?

744. What were things that you did well, and could improve, and how?

745. What are things that you need to improve?

746. Are Offensive Security Certified Professional project team members involved in detailed estimating and scheduling?

747. Do Offensive Security Certified Professional project teams & team members report on status / activities / progress?

748. Are quality inspections and review activities listed in the Offensive Security Certified Professional project schedule(s)?

749. What is the last item a Offensive Security Certified Professional project manager must do to finalize Offensive Security Certified Professional project close-out?

750. Have activity relationships and interdependencies within tasks been adequately identified?

751. Have Offensive Security Certified Professional project team accountabilities & responsibilities been clearly defined?

752. Is a payment system in place with proper reviews and approvals?

2.37 Source Selection Criteria: Offensive Security Certified Professional

753. What should be considered when developing evaluation standards?

754. Do you want to wait until all offerors have been evaluated?

755. Will the technical evaluation factor unnecessarily force the acquisition into a higher-priced market segment?

756. Is this a cost contract?

757. Are there any specific considerations that precludes offers from being selected as the awardee?

758. When is it appropriate to issue a Draft Request for Proposal (DRFP)?

759. Do you ensure you evaluate what you asked for, not what you want to see or expect to see?

760. Do you have a plan to document consensus results including disposition of any disagreement by individual evaluators?

761. Are responses to considerations adequate?

762. What documentation is needed for a tradeoff decision?

763. Comparison of each offers prices to the estimated prices -are there significant differences?

764. Do you consider all weaknesses, significant weaknesses, and deficiencies?

765. Is there collaboration among your evaluators?

766. How can business terms and conditions be improved to yield more effective price competition?

767. What source selection software is your team using?

768. Have all evaluators been trained?

769. What can not be disclosed?

770. What are the limitations on pre-competitive range communications?

771. How do you manage procurement?

772. What is price analysis and when should it be performed?

2.38 Stakeholder Management Plan: Offensive Security Certified Professional

773. Is there a requirements change management processes in place?

774. Have the key elements of a coherent Offensive Security Certified Professional project management strategy been established?

775. Are the Offensive Security Certified Professional project plans updated on a frequent basis?

776. Are the key elements of a Offensive Security Certified Professional project Charter present?

777. Who might be involved in developing a charter?

778. Are formal code reviews conducted?

779. Who is responsible for accepting the reports produced by the process?

780. What records are required (eg purchase orders, agreements)?

781. Are action items captured and managed?

782. Are written status reports provided on a designated frequent basis?

783. Does the Offensive Security Certified Professional

project have a formal Offensive Security Certified Professional project Plan?

784. What is the difference between product and Offensive Security Certified Professional project scope?

785. Are communication systems currently in place appropriate?

786. Is the Offensive Security Certified Professional project sponsor clearly communicating the business case or rationale for why this Offensive Security Certified Professional project is needed?

787. What action will be taken once reports have been received?

788. Are updated Offensive Security Certified Professional project time & resource estimates reasonable based on the current Offensive Security Certified Professional project stage?

789. Are Offensive Security Certified Professional project leaders committed to this Offensive Security Certified Professional project full time?

2.39 Change Management Plan: Offensive Security Certified Professional

790. What method and medium would you use to announce a message?

791. Has a training need analysis been carried out?

792. Which relationships will change?

793. What are the specific target groups/audiences that will be impacted by this change?

794. What are the training strategies?

795. When to start change management?

796. What relationships will change?

797. Is it the same for each of the business units?

798. Identify the risk and assess the significance and likelihood of it occurring and plan the contingency What risks may occur upfront?

799. What prerequisite knowledge or training is required?

800. Who might be able to help you the most?

801. How much change management is needed?

802. What skills, education, knowledge, or work experiences should the resources have for each identified competency?

803. Different application of an existing process?

804. What are the key change management success metrics?

805. When developing your communication plan do you address : When should the given message be communicated?

806. When should a given message be communicated?

807. What do you expect the target audience to do, say, think or feel as a result of this communication?

808. What type of materials/channels will be available to leverage?

809. Who is the audience for change management activities?

3.0 Executing Process Group: Offensive Security Certified Professional

810. Is the program supported by national and/or local organizations?

811. Will outside resources be needed to help?

812. What are the main parts of the scope statement?

813. Is the schedule for the set products being met?

814. Contingency planning. if a risk event occurs, what will you do?

815. What were things that you need to improve?

816. Do schedule issues conflicts?

817. What are the Offensive Security Certified Professional project management deliverables of each process group?

818. How do you measure difficulty?

819. Are decisions made in a timely manner?

820. When do you share the scorecard with managers?

821. Does the Offensive Security Certified Professional project team have enough people to execute the

Offensive Security Certified Professional project plan?

822. What are deliverables of your Offensive Security Certified Professional project?

823. What are crucial elements of successful Offensive Security Certified Professional project plan execution?

824. How could stakeholders negatively impact your Offensive Security Certified Professional project?

825. What areas does the group agree are the biggest success on the Offensive Security Certified Professional project?

826. What is the difference between using brainstorming and the Delphi technique for risk identification?

3.1 Team Member Status Report: Offensive Security Certified Professional

827. Do you have an Enterprise Offensive Security Certified Professional project Management Office (EPMO)?

828. How will resource planning be done?

829. How it is to be done?

830. Does the product, good, or service already exist within your organization?

831. Does your organization have the means (staff, money, contract, etc.) to produce or to acquire the product, good, or service?

832. What specific interest groups do you have in place?

833. How can you make it practical?

834. Are the products of your organizations Offensive Security Certified Professional projects meeting customers objectives?

835. When a teams productivity and success depend on collaboration and the efficient flow of information, what generally fails them?

836. Are your organizations Offensive Security

Certified Professional projects more successful over time?

837. Will the staff do training or is that done by a third party?

838. The problem with Reward & Recognition Programs is that the truly deserving people all too often get left out. How can you make it practical?

839. Why is it to be done?

840. How much risk is involved?

841. How does this product, good, or service meet the needs of the Offensive Security Certified Professional project and your organization as a whole?

842. What is to be done?

843. Does every department have to have a Offensive Security Certified Professional project Manager on staff?

844. Are the attitudes of staff regarding Offensive Security Certified Professional project work improving?

845. Is there evidence that staff is taking a more professional approach toward management of your organizations Offensive Security Certified Professional projects?

3.2 Change Request: Offensive Security Certified Professional

846. Change request coordination ?

847. What type of changes does change control take into account?

848. Who is communicating the change?

849. How many lines of code must be changed to implement the change?

850. Who has responsibility for approving and ranking changes?

851. Are there requirements attributes that are strongly related to the occurrence of defects and failures?

852. Who needs to approve change requests?

853. Are there requirements attributes that can discriminate between high and low reliability?

854. When to submit a change request?

855. Will there be a change request form in use?

856. Are you implementing itil processes?

857. Is it feasible to use requirements attributes as predictors of reliability?

858. Will this change conflict with other requirements changes (e.g., lead to conflicting operational scenarios)?

859. What are the Impacts to your organization?

860. How does a team identify the discrete elements of a configuration?

861. How are changes requested (forms, method of communication)?

862. Who can suggest changes?

863. What is the function of the change control committee?

864. What is a Change Request Form?

865. Screen shots or attachments included in a Change Request?

3.3 Change Log: Offensive Security Certified Professional

866. Is the change backward compatible without limitations?

867. How does this change affect scope?

868. Do the described changes impact on the integrity or security of the system?

869. Will the Offensive Security Certified Professional project fail if the change request is not executed?

870. Who initiated the change request?

871. Is the requested change request a result of changes in other Offensive Security Certified Professional project(s)?

872. Where do changes come from?

873. When was the request approved?

874. When was the request submitted?

875. Is the change request within Offensive Security Certified Professional project scope?

876. Is this a mandatory replacement?

877. Does the suggested change request seem to represent a necessary enhancement to the product?

878. Does the suggested change request represent a desired enhancement to the products functionality?

879. Is the change request open, closed or pending?

880. Should a more thorough impact analysis be conducted?

881. How does this change affect the timeline of the schedule?

882. How does this relate to the standards developed for specific business processes?

883. Is the submitted change a new change or a modification of a previously approved change?

3.4 Decision Log: Offensive Security Certified Professional

884. Who will be given a copy of this document and where will it be kept?

885. What is the line where eDiscovery ends and document review begins?

886. How consolidated and comprehensive a story can you tell by capturing currently available incident data in a central location and through a log of key decisions during an incident?

887. How effective is maintaining the log at facilitating organizational learning?

888. Meeting purpose; why does this team meet?

889. It becomes critical to track and periodically revisit both operational effectiveness; Are you noticing all that you need to, and are you interpreting what you see effectively?

890. What are the cost implications?

891. Which variables make a critical difference?

892. How does an increasing emphasis on cost containment influence the strategies and tactics used?

893. Who is the decisionmaker?

894. Is your opponent open to a non-traditional workflow, or will it likely challenge anything you do?

895. Adversarial environment. is your opponent open to a non-traditional workflow, or will it likely challenge anything you do?

896. With whom was the decision shared or considered?

897. How does the use a Decision Support System influence the strategies/tactics or costs?

898. How does provision of information, both in terms of content and presentation, influence acceptance of alternative strategies?

899. What makes you different or better than others companies selling the same thing?

900. Does anything need to be adjusted?

901. Do strategies and tactics aimed at less than full control reduce the costs of management or simply shift the cost burden?

902. How do you define success?

903. Decision-making process; how will the team make decisions?

3.5 Quality Audit: Offensive Security Certified Professional

904. How does your organization know that its quality of teaching is appropriately effective and constructive?

905. How does your organization know that its management of its ethical responsibilities is appropriately effective and constructive?

906. How does your organization know that its staff entrance standards are appropriately effective and constructive and being implemented consistently?

907. How does your organization know that it is effectively and constructively guiding staff through to timely completion of tasks?

908. How does your organization know that its support services planning and management systems are appropriately effective and constructive?

909. Is your organizational structure established and each positions responsibility defined?

910. Will the evidence likely be sufficient and appropriate?

911. How does your organization know that the quality of its supervisors is appropriately effective and constructive?

912. How do you indicate the extent to which your personnel would be expected to contribute to the work effort?

913. Are there appropriate means for intervening if necessary?

914. How does your organization know that its general support services planning and management systems are appropriately effective and constructive?

915. Are people allowed to contribute ideas?

916. How does your organization know that its teaching activities (and staff learning) are effectively and constructively enhanced by its activities?

917. Is quality audit a prerequisite for program accreditation or program recognition?

918. Are all employees made aware of device defects which may occur from the improper performance of specific jobs?

919. How does your organization know that its systems for providing high quality consultancy services to external parties are appropriately effective and constructive?

920. How does your organization know that its research funding systems are appropriately effective and constructive in enabling quality research outcomes?

921. How does your organization know that its security arrangements are appropriately effective and

constructive?

922. Do all staff have the necessary authority and resources to deliver what is expected of them?

923. Does your organization have set of goals, objectives, strategies and targets that are clearly understood by the Board and staff?

3.6 Team Directory: Offensive Security Certified Professional

924. Process decisions: how well was task order work performed?

925. Who will write the meeting minutes and distribute?

926. Process decisions: are contractors adequately prosecuting the work?

927. What are you going to deliver or accomplish?

928. Who are your stakeholders (customers, sponsors, end users, team members)?

929. Decisions: what could be done better to improve the quality of the constructed product?

930. How and in what format should information be presented?

931. Process decisions: which organizational elements and which individuals will be assigned management functions?

932. Why is the work necessary?

933. When does information need to be distributed?

934. Days from the time the issue is identified?

935. Process decisions: are all start-up, turn over and close out requirements of the contract satisfied?

936. How will the team handle changes?

937. Process decisions: are there any statutory or regulatory issues relevant to the timely execution of work?

938. Who are the Team Members?

939. How does the team resolve conflicts and ensure tasks are completed?

940. How do unidentified risks impact the outcome of the Offensive Security Certified Professional project?

941. Where will the product be used and/or delivered or built when appropriate?

942. Do purchase specifications and configurations match requirements?

3.7 Team Operating Agreement: Offensive Security Certified Professional

943. What types of accommodations will be formulated and put in place for sustaining the team?

944. The method to be used in the decision making process; Will it be consensus, majority rule, or the supervisor having the final say?

945. What is teaming?

946. How will your group handle planned absences?

947. What individual strengths does each team member bring to the group?

948. Do you post meeting notes and the recording (if used) and notify participants?

949. Do you vary your voice pace, tone and pitch to engage participants and gain involvement?

950. Why does your organization want to participate in teaming?

951. Has the appropriate access to relevant data and analysis capability been granted?

952. Conflict resolution: how will disputes and other conflicts be mediated or resolved?

953. Do you record meetings for the already stated unable to attend?

954. What is culture?

955. Communication protocols: how will the team communicate?

956. Are team roles clearly defined and accepted?

957. What are the safety issues/risks that need to be addressed and/or that the team needs to consider?

958. Must your team members rely on the expertise of other members to complete tasks?

959. Do team members reside in more than two countries?

960. What went well?

961. Must your members collaborate successfully to complete Offensive Security Certified Professional projects?

962. Are there more than two native languages represented by your team?

3.8 Team Performance Assessment: Offensive Security Certified Professional

963. Does more radicalness mean more perceived benefits?

964. When does the medium matter?

965. To what degree does the teams work approach provide opportunity for members to engage in open interaction?

966. To what degree are the skill areas critical to team performance present?

967. To what degree can all members engage in open and interactive considerations?

968. What are you doing specifically to develop the leaders around you?

969. How does Offensive Security Certified Professional project termination impact Offensive Security Certified Professional project team members?

970. What do you think is the most constructive thing that could be done now to resolve considerations and disputes about method variance?

971. To what degree do team members understand one anothers roles and skills?

972. Delaying market entry: how long is too long?

973. To what degree do all members feel responsible for all agreed-upon measures?

974. To what degree do team members feel that the purpose of the team is important, if not exciting?

975. Effects of crew composition on crew performance: Does the whole equal the sum of its parts?

976. Can team performance be reliably measured in simulator and live exercises using the same assessment tool?

977. To what degree does the teams work approach provide opportunity for members to engage in results-based evaluation?

978. To what degree are the goals ambitious?

979. Do you give group members authority to make at least some important decisions?

980. To what degree are the members clear on what they are individually responsible for and what they are jointly responsible for?

981. How do you recognize and praise members for contributions?

982. Do you promptly inform members about major developments that may affect them?

3.9 Team Member Performance Assessment: Offensive Security Certified Professional

983. Which training platform formats (i.e., mobile, virtual, videogame-based) were implemented in your effort(s)?

984. What instructional strategies were developed/ incorporated (e.g., direct instruction, indirect instruction, experiential learning, independent study, interactive instruction)?

985. To what degree are sub-teams possible or necessary?

986. To what degree can team members frequently and easily communicate with one another?

987. What are top priorities?

988. How should adaptive assessments be implemented?

989. To what degree can team members meet frequently enough to accomplish the teams ends?

990. Are there any safeguards to prevent intentional or unintentional rating errors?

991. What entity leads the process, selects a potential restructuring option and develops the plan?

992. How are evaluation results utilized?

993. What kinds of performance factors / elements do you use?

994. What are the standards or expectations for success?

995. What steps have you taken to improve performance?

996. Does the rater (supervisor) have the authority or responsibility to tell an employee that the employees performance is unsatisfactory?

997. What are the basic principles and objectives of performance measurement and assessment?

998. Are assessment validation activities performed?

999. What evaluation results do you have?

1000. Is it clear how goals will be accomplished?

1001. To what degree are the teams goals and objectives clear, simple, and measurable?

1002. How is assessment information achieved, stored?

3.10 Issue Log: Offensive Security Certified Professional

1003. Which team member will work with each stakeholder?

1004. Who are the members of the governing body?

1005. Who have you worked with in past, similar initiatives?

1006. In your work, how much time is spent on stakeholder identification?

1007. Who do you turn to if you have questions?

1008. What approaches to you feel are the best ones to use?

1009. How much time does it take to do it?

1010. How were past initiatives successful?

1011. How often do you engage with stakeholders?

1012. Are they needed?

1013. Who is involved as you identify stakeholders?

1014. Are the stakeholders getting the information they need, are they consulted, are concerns addressed?

1015. Is the issue log kept in a safe place?

1016. What is the stakeholders political influence?

1017. Can you think of other people who might have concerns or interests?

1018. What is the stakeholders level of authority?

4.0 Monitoring and Controlling Process Group: Offensive Security Certified Professional

1019. What resources (both financial and non-financial) are available/needed?

1020. How well did the team follow the chosen processes?

1021. How many more potential communications channels were introduced by the discovery of the new stakeholders?

1022. Are the necessary foundations in place to ensure the sustainability of the results of the programme?

1023. Accuracy: what design will lead to accurate information?

1024. Who needs to be involved in the planning?

1025. Is it what was agreed upon?

1026. Did the Offensive Security Certified Professional project team have enough people to execute the Offensive Security Certified Professional project plan?

1027. Propriety: who needs to be involved in the evaluation to be ethical?

1028. Is there sufficient funding available for this?

1029. Is there adequate validation on required fields?

1030. What kinds of things in particular are you looking for data on?

1031. What are the goals of the program?

1032. What communication items need improvement?

1033. Where is the Risk in the Offensive Security Certified Professional project?

1034. In what way has the program come up with innovative measures for problem-solving?

1035. How were collaborations developed, and how are they sustained?

1036. Key stakeholders to work with. How many potential communications channels exist on the Offensive Security Certified Professional project?

4.1 Project Performance Report: Offensive Security Certified Professional

1037. What is the PRS?

1038. To what degree do team members frequently explore the teams purpose and its implications?

1039. To what degree are the goals realistic?

1040. How is the data used?

1041. To what degree does the teams purpose constitute a broader, deeper aspiration than just accomplishing short-term goals?

1042. To what degree is the team cognizant of small wins to be celebrated along the way?

1043. To what degree is there centralized control of information sharing?

1044. To what degree do members articulate the goals beyond the team membership?

1045. To what degree will the approach capitalize on and enhance the skills of all team members in a manner that takes into consideration other demands on members of the team?

1046. Next Steps?

1047. To what degree do team members articulate the teams work approach?

1048. To what degree do the relationships of the informal organization motivate taskrelevant behavior and facilitate task completion?

1049. To what degree does the information network provide individuals with the information they require?

1050. What is the degree to which rules govern information exchange between groups?

1051. What is in it for you?

1052. How can Offensive Security Certified Professional project sustainability be maintained?

1053. To what degree are fresh input and perspectives systematically caught and added (for example, through information and analysis, new members, and senior sponsors)?

1054. To what degree does the team possess adequate membership to achieve its ends?

4.2 Variance Analysis: Offensive Security Certified Professional

1055. Are indirect costs charged to the appropriate indirect pools and incurring organization?

1056. Does the contractor use objective results, design reviews and tests to trace schedule performance?

1057. Are the overhead pools formally and adequately identified?

1058. Are indirect costs accumulated for comparison with the corresponding budgets?

1059. What causes selling price variance?

1060. What business event causes fluctuations?

1061. What is the expected future profitability of each customer?

1062. How do you identify potential or actual overruns and underruns?

1063. What is the total budget for the Offensive Security Certified Professional project (including estimates for authorized and unpriced work)?

1064. Do work packages consist of discrete tasks which are adequately described?

1065. Who are responsible for the establishment of budgets and assignment of resources for overhead performance?

1066. Can the relationship with problem customers be restructured so that there is a win-win situation?

1067. Contemplated overhead expenditure for each period based on the best information currently is available?

1068. Is the entire contract planned in time-phased control accounts to the extent practicable?

1069. Are procedures for variance analysis documented and consistently applied at the control account level and selected WBS and organizational levels at least monthly as a routine task?

1070. Why are standard cost systems used?

1071. What is the performance to date and material commitment?

1072. Who are responsible for overhead performance control of related costs?

4.3 Earned Value Status: Offensive Security Certified Professional

1073. How does this compare with other Offensive Security Certified Professional projects?

1074. Where is evidence-based earned value in your organization reported?

1075. Earned value can be used in almost any Offensive Security Certified Professional project situation and in almost any Offensive Security Certified Professional project environment. it may be used on large Offensive Security Certified Professional projects, medium sized Offensive Security Certified Professional projects, tiny Offensive Security Certified Professional projects (in cut-down form), complex and simple Offensive Security Certified Professional projects and in any market sector. some people, of course, know all about earned value, they have used it for years - but perhaps not as effectively as they could have?

1076. Where are your problem areas?

1077. How much is it going to cost by the finish?

1078. If earned value management (EVM) is so good in determining the true status of a Offensive Security Certified Professional project and Offensive Security Certified Professional project its completion, why is it that hardly any one uses it in information systems related Offensive Security Certified Professional projects?

1079. What is the unit of forecast value?

1080. Validation is a process of ensuring that the developed system will actually achieve the stakeholders desired outcomes; Are you building the right product? What do you validate?

1081. Are you hitting your Offensive Security Certified Professional projects targets?

1082. When is it going to finish?

1083. Verification is a process of ensuring that the developed system satisfies the stakeholders agreements and specifications; Are you building the product right? What do you verify?

4.4 Risk Audit: Offensive Security Certified Professional

1084. What can be measured?

1085. Do you have a clear plan for the future that describes what you want to do and how you are going to do it?

1086. What is happening in other jurisdictions? Could that happen here?

1087. Level of preparation and skill?

1088. Does your organization meet the terms of any contracts with which it is involved?

1089. What are the differences and similarities between strategic and operational risks in your organization?

1090. Are requirements fully understood by the team and customers?

1091. Does the Offensive Security Certified Professional project team have experience with the technology to be implemented?

1092. Have top software and customer managers formally committed to support the Offensive Security Certified Professional project?

1093. Are audit program plans risk-adjusted?

1094. Are staff committed for the duration of the product?

1095. Has an event time line been developed?

1096. Are end-users enthusiastically committed to the Offensive Security Certified Professional project and the system/product to be built?

1097. What are the legal implications of not identifying a complete universe of business risks?

1098. The halo effect in business risk audits: can strategic risk assessment bias auditor judgment about accounting details?

1099. Are regular safety inspections made of buildings, grounds and equipment?

1100. Do requirements put excessive performance constraints on the product?

1101. Do you have a realistic budget and do you present regular financial reports that identify how you are going against that budget?

1102. Is Offensive Security Certified Professional project scope stable?

4.5 Contractor Status Report: Offensive Security Certified Professional

1103. What are the minimum and optimal bandwidth requirements for the proposed soluiton?

1104. Are there contractual transfer concerns?

1105. How is risk transferred?

1106. Who can list a Offensive Security Certified Professional project as organization experience, your organization or a previous employee of your organization?

1107. What was the budget or estimated cost for your organizations services?

1108. How long have you been using the services?

1109. How does the proposed individual meet each requirement?

1110. What was the final actual cost?

1111. If applicable; describe your standard schedule for new software version releases. Are new software version releases included in the standard maintenance plan?

1112. Describe how often regular updates are made to the proposed solution. Are corresponding regular updates included in the standard maintenance plan?

1113. What was the actual budget or estimated cost for your organizations services?

1114. What process manages the contracts?

1115. What was the overall budget or estimated cost?

1116. What is the average response time for answering a support call?

4.6 Formal Acceptance: Offensive Security Certified Professional

1117. Was the Offensive Security Certified Professional project goal achieved?

1118. What function(s) does it fill or meet?

1119. What was done right?

1120. What can you do better next time?

1121. What are the requirements against which to test, Who will execute?

1122. How well did the team follow the methodology?

1123. Who would use it?

1124. General estimate of the costs and times to complete the Offensive Security Certified Professional project?

1125. Was the client satisfied with the Offensive Security Certified Professional project results?

1126. How does your team plan to obtain formal acceptance on your Offensive Security Certified Professional project?

1127. Was the Offensive Security Certified Professional project work done on time, within budget, and according to specification?

1128. Does it do what Offensive Security Certified Professional project team said it would?

1129. Did the Offensive Security Certified Professional project achieve its MOV?

1130. Who supplies data?

1131. What lessons were learned about your Offensive Security Certified Professional project management methodology?

1132. Does it do what client said it would?

1133. What features, practices, and processes proved to be strengths or weaknesses?

1134. Did the Offensive Security Certified Professional project manager and team act in a professional and ethical manner?

1135. What is the Acceptance Management Process?

1136. Is formal acceptance of the Offensive Security Certified Professional project product documented and distributed?

5.0 Closing Process Group: Offensive Security Certified Professional

1137. What was learned?

1138. What areas were overlooked on this Offensive Security Certified Professional project?

1139. What were the desired outcomes?

1140. Is the Offensive Security Certified Professional project funded?

1141. Did you do what you said you were going to do?

1142. How will you do it?

1143. Were decisions made in a timely manner?

1144. How well defined and documented were the Offensive Security Certified Professional project management processes you chose to use?

1145. Did the delivered product meet the specified requirements and goals of the Offensive Security Certified Professional project?

1146. Can the lesson learned be replicated?

1147. What is the amount of funding and what Offensive Security Certified Professional project phases are funded?

1148. Did the Offensive Security Certified Professional project team have the right skills?

1149. What could be done to improve the process?

1150. What were things that you did very well and want to do the same again on the next Offensive Security Certified Professional project?

1151. What could have been improved?

5.1 Procurement Audit: Offensive Security Certified Professional

1152. In a competitive dialogue, were solutions proposed or confidential information given by a candidate not revealed to others without his/her express agreement?

1153. Are there any complaints of the suppliers and/or end-users?

1154. Are there procedures governing how sales and use tax will be handled (ordering in state versus ordering out of state)?

1155. Has the expected benefits from realisation of the procurement Offensive Security Certified Professional project been calculated?

1156. Are internal control systems in place?

1157. Are idle funds invested, and is interest distributed to the various activity accounts at least annually?

1158. Are information gathered to produce knowledge about procured goods and services, prices paid and supplier performance?

1159. Which are necessary components of a financial audit report under the Single Audit Act?

1160. Were additional works strictly necessary for the

completion of performance under the contract?

1161. Are sub-criteria clearly indicated?

1162. Are the purchase order forms designed for efficient and simple completion?

1163. Are regulations and protective measures in place to avoid corruption?

1164. Are the internal control systems operational?

1165. Is it tested periodically, whether your organizations way of handling tasks is competitive in relation to price and quality?

1166. Are travel expenditures monitored to determine that they are in line with other employees and reasonable for the area of travel?

1167. Are procedures established so that vendors with poor quality or late delivery are identified to eliminate additional dealings with that vendor?

1168. Has your organization fulfilled its obligations related to the payment of social security contributions and taxes?

1169. Do all requests for materials, supplies, and services require supervisors authorization?

1170. Are all initial purchase contracts made by the purchasing organization?

1171. Do at least two people have custodial responsibilities for negotiable checks (one checking on the other)?

5.2 Contract Close-Out: Offensive Security Certified Professional

1172. What is capture management?

1173. How does it work?

1174. Was the contract complete without requiring numerous changes and revisions?

1175. Are the signers the authorized officials?

1176. Change in attitude or behavior?

1177. Was the contract sufficiently clear so as not to result in numerous disputes and misunderstandings?

1178. Parties: who is involved?

1179. Have all contracts been closed?

1180. Has each contract been audited to verify acceptance and delivery?

1181. Parties: Authorized?

1182. How/when used ?

1183. Why Outsource?

1184. How is the contracting office notified of the automatic contract close-out?

1185. Have all contract records been included in the Offensive Security Certified Professional project archives?

1186. Change in knowledge?

1187. Was the contract type appropriate?

1188. Have all acceptance criteria been met prior to final payment to contractors?

1189. What happens to the recipient of services?

1190. Change in circumstances?

1191. Have all contracts been completed?

5.3 Project or Phase Close-Out: Offensive Security Certified Professional

1192. In preparing the Lessons Learned report, should it reflect a consensus viewpoint, or should the report reflect the different individual viewpoints?

1193. What was expected from each stakeholder?

1194. In addition to assessing whether the Offensive Security Certified Professional project was successful, it is equally critical to analyze why it was or was not fully successful. Are you including this?

1195. Was the schedule met?

1196. Who controlled key decisions that were made?

1197. When and how were information needs best met?

1198. What are they?

1199. What can you do better next time, and what specific actions can you take to improve?

1200. What hierarchical authority does the stakeholder have in your organization?

1201. What is the information level of detail required for each stakeholder?

1202. What was the preferred delivery mechanism?

1203. What benefits or impacts does the stakeholder group expect to obtain as a result of the Offensive Security Certified Professional project?

1204. Does the lesson educate others to improve performance?

1205. Is the lesson based on actual Offensive Security Certified Professional project experience rather than on independent research?

1206. Planned completion date?

1207. Were cost budgets met?

1208. Does the lesson describe a function that would be done differently the next time?

1209. What security considerations needed to be addressed during the procurement life cycle?

1210. What information did each stakeholder need to contribute to the Offensive Security Certified Professional projects success?

5.4 Lessons Learned: Offensive Security Certified Professional

1211. Did the Offensive Security Certified Professional project management methodology work?

1212. How closely did deliverables match what was defined within the Offensive Security Certified Professional project Scope?

1213. How satisfied are you with your involvement in the development and/or review of the Offensive Security Certified Professional project Scope during Offensive Security Certified Professional project Initiation and Planning?

1214. How effective were the communications materials in providing and orienting team members about the details of the Offensive Security Certified Professional project?

1215. How effective were the techniques used to prepare you and your organization for the impact of the changes brought about by the product or service produced by the Offensive Security Certified Professional project?

1216. How clear were you on your role in the Offensive Security Certified Professional project?

1217. Was the control overhead justified?

1218. Were quality procedures built into the Offensive

Security Certified Professional project?

1219. Was sufficient time allocated to review Offensive Security Certified Professional project deliverables?

1220. How to write up the lesson identified – how will you document the results of your analysis corresponding that you have an li ready to take the next step in the ll process?

1221. How was the Offensive Security Certified Professional project controlled?

1222. Was the necessary hardware, software, accommodation etc available?

1223. How well prepared were you to receive Offensive Security Certified Professional project deliverables?

1224. How effective was the acceptance management process?

1225. Was sufficient advance training conducted and/or information provided to enable the already stated affected by the changes to adjust to and accommodate them?

1226. Was the change control process properly implemented to manage changes to cost, scope, schedule, or quality?

1227. How well were expectations met regarding the frequency and content of information that was conveyed to by the Offensive Security Certified Professional project Manager?

1228. How actively and meaningfully were stakeholders involved in the Offensive Security Certified Professional project?

1229. How effective was the architecture/system design process?

1230. Under what legal authority did your organization head and program manager direct your organization and Offensive Security Certified Professional project?

Index

explicit 206
explicitly   135
exploit 72, 77, 100-101, 107
exploiting   34, 60
explore   63, 259
explored   221
expose 124
exposure   102, 218
exposures   36
express 273
expressed   154
extent 13, 32, 73, 151, 245, 262
external   28, 32, 85, 101, 120, 127, 132, 171, 212, 214, 220, 245
externally   64, 133
facilitate   13, 24, 87, 260
facilities   159
facing 20, 130, 220
factor 158, 228
factors 45-46, 74, 137, 146, 151, 178, 198, 254
failed 42
failing 107
failure 42, 115, 130, 166, 224
failures 238
fairly   36
falling 173
familiar 10
families 196
fashion 1, 32, 216
favorable   171
feasible   45, 64, 137, 198, 238
feature 11
features   154, 217, 270
feedback   2, 12, 29, 37, 42, 143
fewest 123
fields   258
figure   52
Filter   204
finalize 197, 227
finalized   15
financial   48, 56, 65, 77, 114, 148, 216, 257, 266, 273
finding 187
fingertips   11

requested   1, 77, 143, 239-240
requests   238, 274
require 34, 50, 94, 182, 193, 218, 220, 260, 274
required   24, 27-28, 30-31, 34, 36, 72, 78, 144, 159, 174-176,
187, 189, 192, 205, 211-212, 219-220, 222, 230, 232, 258, 278
requires   46
requiring   147, 276
research   112, 178, 187, 245, 279
reserved   1
reserves   171
reside 250
resolution   65, 249
resolve 248, 251
resolved   191, 195, 216, 249
resource   4-5, 84, 156, 172, 182, 184-185, 194, 212, 231, 236
resources   2, 10, 23, 28, 39, 54, 71, 78, 83, 87, 98, 102, 116,
119, 139, 143-144, 148, 166, 173, 175-177, 181, 185, 187, 189, 192,
194-195, 198, 208, 226, 233-234, 246, 257, 262
respect   1
respective   73, 150
respond   127, 151
responded   14
response   21, 53, 83-84, 87-88, 93, 268
responses   228
responsive   190, 198
restricted   93, 123
result   60, 72, 77, 151, 171, 199, 205, 215, 233, 240, 276, 279
resulted   85
resulting   56
results 10, 32, 35, 43, 57, 67-69, 72, 74, 76-79, 83, 85, 144, 150-
152, 177, 186, 192, 198, 205, 209, 228, 254, 257, 261, 269, 281
retain 95, 134, 138
retained   110, 134
retaining   187
retention   187
retested   107
retesting   25
retrospect   121
return 42, 77, 180, 206, 222
returned   39
reveal 120
revealed   273
revenue   46, 49-50

should 8, 23, 25, 32, 38, 49, 52, 54, 57, 63, 70, 74-75, 77-78, 80,
83, 88, 93, 107, 110, 116, 118, 126-127, 129-131, 136, 144, 147,
149-151, 153-154, 157, 166, 175, 177, 189, 196, 210, 219-222, 224,
228-229, 233, 241, 247, 253, 278
showing   151
signature   107-109
signatures   104, 128, 182
signed 163
signers 276
similar 28, 31, 57-58, 76, 86, 148, 174, 177, 221-222, 255
simple 118, 254, 263, 274
simply 10, 12, 243
simulate   132
simulated   47, 85
simulator   252
single 65, 112, 273
single-use   8
situation   21, 41, 219, 262-263
situations   132
skeptical   136
skills   25-26, 45, 47, 100, 127, 131, 178, 187, 201, 211, 216, 233,
251, 259, 272
smaller 151
smallest   24, 77
social   136, 140, 225, 274
software   24, 44, 102-103, 133, 139, 157, 166, 212, 216, 229,
265, 267, 281
solicit   29, 186
soluiton   267
solution   45, 64-65, 67-69, 71-72, 74-76, 78-79, 82, 267
solutions   45, 47, 50, 68, 73-76, 80, 273
Someone   8
something   121, 153
Sometimes   45, 50
sought 148
source 6, 44, 108, 120, 140, 224, 228-229
sources   30, 58, 63, 67
special 83, 146
specific   10, 23, 32, 34, 37, 108, 110, 120, 167, 174, 176,
178, 180, 182, 184, 186, 191, 200, 228, 232, 236, 241, 245, 278
specified   135, 171, 224, 271
spoken 117
sponsor   20, 153, 164, 213, 231